War, Reconstruction and Redemption on Red River

The Memoirs of Dosia Williams Moore

War, Reconstruction and Redemption on Red River

The Memoirs of Dosia Williams Moore

Edited by
Carol Wells

McGINTY PUBLICATIONS

DEPARTMENT OF HISTORY
LOUISIANA TECH UNIVERSITY
1990
Ruston, Louisiana

Printed in the United States of America

Library of Congress Catalog Number: 90-60556
ISBN 0-940231-06-9

Contents

"Whether the impression was well founded or not, it existed in the minds of the people, and it was upon that impression that they acted.*

Robert P. Hunter, Rapides Parish

*U.S., Congress, House, *Report of the Select Committee on that Portion of the President's Message Relating to the Condition of the South. Testimony Taken by the Committee*, 43rd Cong., 2nd sess., 1873, Report 261, Part 3:533.

Foreword

Dosia Williams Lewis Moore lived in Louisiana's Rapides and northern Natchitoches Parishes during and after the Civil War. She was born in South Carolina and at age three years came to Louisiana with her parents. Through her observations one senses the emotions and views the problems which, even in childhood, she and her loved ones faced.

Dosia kept herself out of her stories. All one knows of her is that which is necessary to set the scene for her stories. Her name, her age, her husbands' names, the name of her son, or the genealogy of her family are not mentioned. Why the Moores left their house Loyd Hall, or what problems she faced, are omitted.

She is seen as a loving, aged lady who was grateful for attention, but whose thoughts turned always to her friends. Luckily, among those friends were Caroline Dormon and Cammie Henry. They preserved the tales they heard from Miss Dosia. Miss Dormon preserved Miss Dosia's memoirs so faithfully that we can almost hear her voice as she lets friend and foe, black and white, speak through her. Mrs. Henry pursued and preserved facts; she had Miss Dosia's written comments on plantations and planters' families typed and bound. Miss Dormon planned a book; Mrs. Henry preserved materials for future historians. This book is the result of both women's efforts. Besides the pages Miss Dormon wanted to include, there exists in the collections of the Archives Division of the Watson Library at Northwestern State University of Louisiana Miss Dosia's additional memoirs and correspondence. More than half a century ago these were probably considered to be too sensitive to be made public. I have included much of the omitted material, such as the murder of Lloyd Shorter. Miss Dormon abbreviated or changed the wording in other tales. I have included the full text and the original words wherever possible (as in the story of the feud). Sometimes two or more versions of one incident exist, probably often retold to Caroline Dormon and Virginia Miller as they sat with Miss Dosia on a summer's evening on the gallery of the old house at Briarwood; each time the story was amplified with additional details, thereby enhancing the validity of the account. One tale with multiple versions is the coming of General Banks' troops in his first raid on Alexandria. Here I have attempted to include all details by weaving together sentences and paragraphs from each version. In the original plan of the book, tales told to Miss Dosia by her father and her husband were not to be included. However they have been added.

Dosia had a remarkable memory. In the few instances where a discrepancy between her tale and written history exists, her tale stands unchanged, but the footnote will provide additional facts. Other footnotes corroborate her stories or give additional, often previously unpublished, details of local history.

I am indebted to Philip C. Cook, Louisiana Tech University, for reading the manuscript and to Ralph D. Pierce, Louisiana Tech University, for the map on the inside book cover.

Carol Wells

War, Reconstruction and Redemption on Red River

The Memoirs of Dosia Williams Moore

I

From South Carolina to Louisiana

Oh Maria, hoo-oo-oo-hoo-oo, hoo-oo-oo-oo-oo
I'm gwine away tomorrow
I'm gwine way to leave you, hoo-oo-oo-hoo-oo

There is not the slightest doubt that I had heard this plaintive little "hollerin'-song" all the three years of my life, but it seemed to me then that it had been made up just to fit the occasion. We *were* going away—to far-off Louisiana. It had been decided. Everyone spoke of Louisiana as "Way out West." We should probably be scalped by Indians, I thought. This was exciting. Sister and I would go out to our favorite mimosa tree, and play Indians. I enjoyed it until it came to scalping my doll, then I screamed lustily.

1

Sometimes I was very sad over it. I felt this the day I went to watch them "run" the lumber from the mill for the last time. I can still see the little pond (it looked enormous to me then) with the dark water, the surface dotted with planks. These were lashed together somehow, into rough rafts. The sluice-gate opened, then came the excitement of guiding the rafts through. They had to pass under a bridge, and I always squealed with delight when big black Tobe leaped nimbly off, ran the length of the bridge, then sprang on a raft again. Pere said Tobe would take the timbers down the Edisto [River] and up the coast to Charleston, which sounded very magnificent to me. I looked up to Tobe for being allowed to take this mysterious journey alone.

We were going just as soon as Pere [Dosia Moore's father] could "make arrangements." These arrangements occupied months, for it was December before we were actually ready to go. I understood only that Pere and an old friend and neighbor were "going in together," and that both were going to become very rich as a result. Even the Negroes seemed pleased over the prospect. Only in late afternoons their songs seemed to take on a little deeper note of sadness.

There was really nothing to mar my delight, for my whole world was moving with me. It probably did not occur to me to wonder what it would be like if Eddie, Nannie, Allen, and English had not been going, too. As it finally worked out, however, they did not actually go along, but came later, and it was three years before I saw them again. It was decided that my father should take the Negro hands on ahead, and have the land cleared and in readiness when his friend came. Of course Pere would take his family.

At last it was decided that my father should go on horseback with the Negroes and loaded wagons, while Mere [Dosia Moore's mother], Sister, and I traveled more comfortably. Mr. [Edward L.] Patterson said that he would go at the same time and look after us. Pere started some time before we did. On a December day we left, but by some strange freak of memory, I cannot recall our actual departure. I suppose there was so much confusion that no one incident made a sufficiently vivid impression on my baby mind. Stranger still, I do not remember the ride on the train—my first!

For me, the journey begins at some point on a river (my mother has since told me that it was the Alabama). We were on a steamboat, and it was night. There was a great stir on the boat. They had stopped to take on cotton, I heard a man say. High overhead were things that resembled big baskets, and these were filled with blazing fat pine torches. I could see drops of hot pitch dropping, dropping. A Negro man on the bluff would call, "Heigh-ho! The one on deck would answer, "Hi-yi!" And then down would come a bale of cotton, rolling and bouncing, to bump onto the deck. The flickering torches cast an eerie light. It is very vivid in my mind. Possibly I was frightened.

All the ladies and gentlemen on the boat were very grand, and Mere kept Sister and me dressed up in all our frills every day. I rather enjoyed this at first, but it soon began to be very irksome to a wild little filly who had had the run of a plantation, and was in the habit of climbing trees and riding stick horses with the little Negroes. One day Mere left us in the charge of my beloved Crecy, and in turn left Crecy under the eye of a laundress below [below deck—inside the steamboat]. The laundress evidently fascinated Crecy so much that her attention wandered, and Sister and I found some stairs that beckoned us. They went down into the fuel room. It was filled with good old smutty pine-knots. Whether or not these smelled of home I cannot say, but we were soon playing happily among them. When Mere missed, and finally found us, she almost fainted when she saw our once-white dresses. Crecy burst into tears, and the laundry woman saved the day by insisting that it was her fault and that she would "do up" the dresses "good as new."

Only one other thing stands out clearly in my mind, and that is the songs that were sung on the boat—constantly, it seems in memory. I have the impression, too, that everybody sang them, though probably it was usually the deckhands. Surely Crecy must have taught them to Sister and me, for I can still recall the words. One ran like this:

> When I was young I used to wait
> On Massa's table and hand de plate,
> Pass de bottle when he was dry,
> And brush away de blue-tail fly.

"Hog-eye" was even more popular:

> Massa fed me on hog-eye meat
> As long as he was able;
> And when de hog-eye meat give out
> He fed me de leg o' de table.

> Oh, git along, hog-eye, git along hog-eye,
> Hog-eye, ladies, hog-eye.

> When he went to New Orleans
> He tuck me for a waiter.
> There he married a Yankee gal,
> And damn 'er soul I hate 'er.

> Refrain.

I know that Sister learned "Run, Nigger, Run" for one day she was so indiscreet as to sing it in Mere's presence, and was severely reprimanded—harmless though it seems to me now. It was almost endless, but this is what I remember:

4

Nigger and white man
Playin' seben-up,
Nigger won de money
But he skeered to pick it up.

Run, nigger, run, de pat-a-rol'll git you,
Run, nigger, run, for it's almost day.
Nigger run, nigger flew,
Nigger to' his shirt in two,
Run, nigger, run, de pat-a-rol'll git you,
Run, nigger, run, for it's almost day.

We must have passed along the Gulf Coast to New Orleans, up the Mississippi River, then up the Red, but of this I cannot be sure. I can remember only that it was a delightful journey. We were much petted by the captain and crew. Sister seldom got into mischief, as she was always the perfect little lady. Although just eighteen months older than I, she tried to restrain my wild spirits.

Pere was waiting for us at Alexandria, on Red River, and there we joined him for the trip overland to the hills of North Louisiana. That trip is as vivid in my mind as if it had ended yesterday. It was one long glorious picnic to two little girls who had been dressed in their best for so long on the boat. What an adventure to ride on one of the loaded wagons! The great unending forests, the deer grazing on the green hillsides, the wild turkeys thundering up in front of the wagon, and all day long, big black Richard shifting his lines and singing, "Massa Got a House in Baltimore," his singing interspersed with an occasional lazy "gid-dap!"[1]

1. "Massa's got a house in Baltimore / Big glass windows, too-di-o! / Massa's got a house in Baltimore / Three, four stories high / Three, four stories high." Dormon Collection, Archives Division, Northwestern State University, Natchitoches, La. (hereafter cited NSU).

Just before sundown, Pere and Mere would begin looking for a camping place. This was somehow very exciting. There must be a good spring, or a clear, cold stream; high, dry ground nearby, and plenty of trees. The spring was seldom hard to find, the trees, never. Our excitement ran high when Pere said, "Well, I believe this is what we are looking for." A new place for Sister and me to explore! First thing, a Negro man was detailed to gather firewood, never a difficult task. Soon he would have a roaring campfire of rich pine-knots and dry oak limbs. He would then pile up enough wood to keep the fire going all night. One of the Negro women would prepare supper. I shall never forget the deliciousness of those meals. During the day Pere would always kill a wild turkey, some quails, squirrels, or maybe even a deer and we would feast at supper. Hot hoecakes cooked on a covered skillet, sweet potatoes roasted in the ashes, the smell of broiling meat and oak-wood-smoke—Oh, feast of the gods! And, oh, heavenly sleep that followed—lulled to rest by the surf-like roar of the longleaf pines and the demoniacal voices of laughing-owls.

Everything was not always perfection, even in my baby mind. Late one afternoon we came to a large creek that had to be crossed. A Frenchman came up on the other side and my father asked him if the ford was safe. The man spoke rather brokenly, and whether Pere understood him correctly I do not know. Anyhow, the first wagon, in which Mere, Sister, and I were riding, turned over in midstream. Something fell on top of me, and Pere dashed up on his horse just in time to drag me out by one foot. It was terrible. Everything was wet, and it was raw, cold weather. The Frenchman was very kind, and urged us to go to his house nearby and spend the night. We went, and there I had my first "dram." While our things were drying out that night, a little black-eyed girl took Sister and me off in a room to ourselves. "Do you want a dram?" she asked. "It's good." We had no idea what a dram was, but it sounded good, so we said "Yes." She produced a dark-blue glass bottle, and poured us each a swallow of raw whiskey. We were almost strangled. When we reported this to Mere, she warned us against all drams in the future.

My first real tragedy occurred on this trip. The episode of the overturned wagon was a happy incident by comparison. I cared very little for my own clothes, though I always admired those of my pretty sister. However, I owned one garment which, for some occult reason, was very precious in my eyes. This was a little pink merino jacket, trimmed in black silk braid. Though I loved it, I could not be burdened with the care of it. In romping about the campfire one night I threw it on a bush. Somehow Mere overlooked it. Alas, the next morning it was a sad memory—the mules had chewed it up! It had been thrown down within the circle of the stake-ropes. I have never really set my heart on a garment since.

At last we reached the Promised Land. This consisted of beautifully wooded sand hills, one fairly comfortable house, and several cabins. A golden pine-woods stream formed one boundary of the plantation. The plantation existed chiefly in Pere's mind, for only about twenty acres of land had been cleared.

Our first day at home stands clear in my mind. In the long trek from South Carolina, only necessities and a few of our most precious treasures could be brought. It so happened that tables fitted into neither category. Pere said we could get whatever we needed after we arrived. He and Mr. Patterson had gone out to look over the neighborhood, and had brought Mr. Prothro home for midday dinner![2] Manlike, he did not realize

2. Govan Williams, 32, S.C.; Mary R., 27, S.C.; Theodosia, 3, S.C.; Edward L. Patterson, 40, planter, S.C. (No. 158-158); Joshua Prothro, 56, planter; Emeline, 45 (No. 159-159); Asa M. Prothro, 38, Gin Agent, Ga.; Frances A., 8; Caroline R., 7 (No. 160-160); James E. Prothro, 36, planter, Ga.; Sarah, 30; William, 10; Eugenia, 8; Alfred, 5; (illegible), 3, M; (illegible), 1 month, F (No.

the difficulties of having guests in the midst of the present confusion. Mere was equal to the occasion. First, a table.

"Richard, you take down that door between the dining-room and kitchen. We don't really need it now." When the door was taken down, placed on four blocks, and spread with a snowy linen cloth it made a splendid table!

"But Mum Charlotte, what on earth are to going to have for dinner? I hate to have just meat and bread." Mum Charlotte chuckled delightedly, "I got somep'n fo' dinner!" She bustled out, and in a few minutes returned with a checked apron full of collard greens! "You 'member dat fine garden we passed back up de road? Well, when I sot eyes on it, I says, 'Charlotte, we's gwine hab colla'd greens fo' dinner!' I made 'em stop de wagon, and went in an ax 'em. De lady says, 'Des go he'p yo'sef!' An' I done so."

Those collards had been through the freezing required to make them tender, and I shall never forget how good they were. For weeks we had been on the road, with no fresh vegetables. I must say that Mr. Prothro seemed to enjoy Mere's hot biscuits and famous peach preserves more than he did the collards. At any rate the dinner was a success, and Pere never suspected what consternation he had caused by bringing home a guest the very first day. As I look back, I cannot recall a single occasion on which Mere failed to rise to an emergency.

We were very sad when Mr. Patterson went back to South Carolina, but it was not long before we children, at least, began to feel at home in the new country.

161-161); H. Readhimer, 52, planter; John, 29, S.C.; Charles, 26, S.C.; William, 20, S.C.; Larance, 16, S.C.; William, 13, S.C. (No. 162-162). There is no explanation why Sister was omitted from the Govan Williams household or why the Readhimer household listed two sons named William. Federal Population Census: 1860. Eighth Census of the U.S. Natchitoches Parish, La., p. 447 (hereafter cited Census, Natchitoches Parish). Wm. M. Prothro, 31, planter, S.C.; Elizabeth M., 28; (illegible), 70, M; Sarah, 7; Wm. H., 2; Sarah Johnson, 21 (No. 983-983); L. E. Prothro, overseer, S.C.; Lucy P.; Solomon (No. 984-984). Census: 1870, Natchitoches Parish, La., p. 113.

I can recall only happiness in this first year in the Louisiana sand hills. The central figure of my life at that time was a Negro nurse, Crecy. She was my key to happiness. My baby mind held only one bitterness against her. My fat little legs were slow, and sometimes Sister and the four small Negro girls, Crecy, Minnow, Emma, and Juliann, planned expeditions in which I was counted out. On these occasions, Crecy would heartlessly say, "Well, jes' wait 'till I puts de baby to sleep." Speechless with disappointment, I would determine that I was *not* going to sleep, but Crecy would urge "des set in my lap a little while, den." Gently she would begin to rock her body back and forth, and croon an indescribable song. The words were few, but there was black magic in that song:

> Bye yo' Bye, Bye yo' bye, Bye yo' bye, pretty baby!
> You shall ride in a golden gig,
> Same as pretty little Martha!
> Bye yo' bye, Bye yo' bye, Go to sleep li'l baby!

The next thing I knew, I waked up in bed, and my playmates were vanished.

The most glorious adventure of all was the time I went to the Negro party with Crecy. She cajoled until my mother consented. It was right in the neighborhood, in the daytime, and she knew that Crecy would guard me with her life. Crecy was a slim, pretty girl, and quite popular. I can see her yet as she swung backwards and forwards, round and round, in the "singin' games." A brown gallant would dance forward, singing:

> Miss Crecy she's a nice young gal,
> Miss Crecy she's a lady,
> Miss Crecy she can wheel and turn,
> And kiss the one that's dancing!

Poor Crecy had to wheel and turn with a fat little girl of three swinging to her skirts! Then it was the girl's turn and Crecy would sing:

Mr. Tobin he's a nice young man,
Mr. Tobin he's a gent'man,
Mr. Tobin he can wheel and turn
And kiss the one that's dancing.

I shared in everything but the kiss! Alas for my happiness! Joy could never last. Pere happened to be riding by and what was his horror on seeing his baby at a "nigger party"! Without a word, he picked me up, got on his horse and rode home. He looked a little sheepish when Mere told him a little crisply that she had given Crecy permission to take me!

My father was a god to me, but, godlike, he often interrupted my dearest pleasures. There was the day I was behind the kitchen stove eating potliker. The cook often kept the babies of the women who were working in the field. On this day there were three small black urchins to be fed, so Mum Charlotte prepared a pan of turnip-green potlicker and cornbread and put it on the floor for them. Never did anything look so delicious to me! I slipped around, crawled behind the stove—where I could reach the pan—and dipped into the communal dish. Oh, but it was good! Then a long shadow fell across the floor. It was Pere! In trying to scramble farther out of sight I attracted his attention—and my part of the feast was over.

In our new home we had few neighbors, and most of them lived as much as ten miles away. Two families that lived within a mile were kind and hospitable while we were getting settled. They sent offerings of vegetables, eggs, and milk until we could get cows and chickens and make a garden.

One Sunday afternoon we had all walked over to Mrs.

Readhimer's for a little visit. When we started home, she filled a big bottle with sweet milk for us to take home. I plead with Mere to let me carry it, and finally she consented. Strutting proudly ahead with the bottle clasped in my arms, I was suddenly confronted by two horsemen. When they stopped, I felt it to be a threat. I drew myself up, "My Mere told me to tote this bottle of milk!" I bristled. One of the men put his hand over his mouth. The other one spoke, "Well you hang to it, Sissy!" he said. "Don't you let anybody take it away from you!"

When they came up with Pere and Mere, I heard them all laughing, but I did not know what the joke was.

Most of my highlights are rose colored. In the summer, after the crop was "laid by," a big camp-fish was planned. Our family and all of the close neighbors (that is, those within ten miles) went in wagons down to Drake's Salt Works, about thirteen miles away. This was a wonderful place to all the country roundabout. There was a great salt deposit, and nobody knew how many years salt had been manufactured there. The Natchitoches Indians had gotten it and traded to other tribes. From them the white men had learned of the deposit, but they had improved on the method of the Indians by boring an artesian well. This furnished a continuous flow of strong brine, and great kettles were brought for evaporating it.

Strange to say, Saline, the big creek which flowed through this region, was not at all briny, though there were other deposits higher up along the stream. It was clear, and filled with fish. In the cool of the day all who could hold a rod repaired to this creek, coming in time for the Negroes to clean the fish and fry them for dinner. Perch and bass (trout, we called them) fresh from the water were delicious, and how everybody did eat! The high-piled platters were soon emptied. The Negroes preferred catfish, and set out hooks at night to catch them.

There was a long rest under the big trees after dinner, then those who desired went out again and caught fish for supper. Of course there were plenty of other dainties for those who tired of fish. After supper, everyone sat about a big bonfire and sang and told stories. Some of the men told tall ones about hunting, and I can remember yet how my hair rose when Mr. Prothro told about fire-hunting one night, shining a supposed deer's eyes, when the eyes began moving right up a big tree!

It was a great time. Even here, though, I was not free of Crecy's sorcery, but every day was magiced [*sic*] with the Golden Gig song. In the mornings when Mere wanted to go out fishing, there came Crecy's hateful formula, "Yes'm, des wait till I puts de baby to sleep." One day I was compensated. It had been a full day. I had waded in the shallow water on the salt flats, and had fallen down, until every garment I had along was soaked. I was reduced to my last—a little thin blue apron. I was very heavy-hearted, as everyone had gone fishing and left me with the Negro children. Crecy was getting me to sleep, when a man rode up. To my joy it was our beloved Mr. Patterson, just back from South Carolina! He took me in his arms and told me all the news of the children. What bliss to have this surprise, and to know that I was the first to see him! I told him that they had all gone off and left me, and that I had to go to sleep. He said that he was sleepy, too, and would I let him lie on my pallet with me? He was tired out from his long trip, and stretched out in the shade. When the fishermen returned, they found us both fast asleep on the pallet. That is the only nap I can remember that held no bitterness.

II

War Comes to Red River

Memory takes strange liberties with my past. Much as I loved the sand hills, I cannot remember when we left them and moved to the river. Pere had not been very much elated over his success in the hills, and the rich river country beckoned. There was a fine opportunity open to him on Red River—so to Red River we went.

It may be that nothing particularly exciting happened to me in the next year and a half; or it may be that it was blotted out by the cataclysm that followed—WAR. To me, of course, war only meant that my father, and the fathers of all the other children, went away; that our mothers were sad most of the time, and that life became changeful, uncertain, and exciting.

I remember the day Pere came home and announced that he had enlisted in the cavalry.[1] I thought it sounded fine, and wanted to join the cavalry, too. I was surprised when Mere and Sister cried. But much more exciting was the day his company went away. All the ladies gathered in Alexandria to see them off. The soldiers looked very grand on their prancing horses. They were dashing and gay, and rode up on the levee to fire a farewell salute. I was jumping up and down and waving my lit-

1. Govan Williams, Pvt. Co. G, 2nd La. Cav., Enlisted June or Aug. 21, 1862, Alexandria, La. July & Aug. 1863 absent, sick at hospital; Roll of prisoners of war of detachments of regiments, CSA. Paroled Natchitoches, La., June 21, 1865. Res. Natchitoches Parish, La. Andrew B. Booth, *Records of Louisiana Confederate Soldiers and the Louisiana Commands* (New Orleans, 1920), p. 1095.

tle handkerchief with all my might, when a scream at my side whirled me about. A lady fell in a faint at my feet.

Almost as vivid in my mind as the farewell to the soldiers was our finding of Tom Green on the way home. He was by the side of the dusty road, a little starved kitten, wailing piteously. We gathered him up and took him home. He grew enormously, and we named him Tom Green, after a Confederate General.[2]

Our strange new lives moved swiftly. We soon became used to talk of fighting and death. We had heard awful stories of what the Yankees would do when they came, and our childish minds were filled with hatred and fear. Aunt Margaret, a dear old colored woman who had long reigned over the children's playroom, told us ghastly tales of battle and murder and sudden death, and for a long time we shuddered at the awful stories. We expected the awful horde to come to our home, and we pictured all sorts of horrors that would come upon us when the Yankees came. [General Nathaniel] Banks [the Union Army Commander] was one of the ogres who led these creatures. After many weeks passed and nothing bad had overtaken us, our fears subsided, and we resumed our delightful playing under the China[berry] trees.

One day word came that "Banks is coming."[3] His army was at Alexandria, and was going to march up Red River. We chil-

2. Thomas Green, born 1814, died at Blair's Landing, April 14, 1862. W. T. Shaw to Dr. Milton Dunn, Melrose Collection, Archives Division, NSU: "I was present at Blair's Landing charging the enemy gunboats near where Gen. Tom Green was killed. One half of his skull was taken off by a shell. As our brigade retreated from that engagement generally known as the gunboat fight, Gen. Green's body was carried out on horseback held on by two comrades." *The National Cyclopaedia of American Biography*, IV, 362.

3. General Nathaniel P. Banks, who had over 40,000 soldiers in his Department of the Gulf, invaded the Red River Valley. Alexandria surrendered May 9, 1863. Sue Eakin, *Rapides Parish History*, p. 47. "Camp near Alexandria La May 27th 1863. I only saw Alexandria from the River. It is a beautiful and quite a large place. The feds did verry little damage to the town. They destroyed the foundry and some shops, burned up some cotton houses

dren had been playing under the trees all the long, sunny afternoon. Panic followed the announcement.

Our family and three others gathered at the home of Mrs. Magruder. She had one Negro man and his wife who were true to their mistress, Uncle Robert and Aunt Margaret, and one boy, Bose. The other Negroes were in open revolt, refused to work, and were very insolent.[4] The only white man in the whole neighborhood was Mr. W—, the elderly tutor who taught the children of Dr. Luckett at their nearby plantation. There was much discussion as to what was to be done. Some advocated fleeing to the pine woods and hiding there. At last, though, it was decided to send for the tutor, and get the only possible masculine advice. Bose was dispatched with a note requesting Mr. W— to please come down to see them, as they were afraid of the approaching army. He wrote that he would come to see them after supper; so great preparations were made for a private interview.

A room in the back of the house was prepared, candles lighted, and doors and windows closed. The children, though anxious to be present, were herded into the playroom in a wing far removed from this temporary "council chamber."

Years later my mother laughingly told me what happened that day. In due time Mr. W— arrived with all the pomp he

---

& fencing. But in the Parish they destroyed all the crops, stole all the negroes, horses, mules, cotton, sugar, molasses etc. They did immense damage to the Parish." Elijah P. Petty, *Journey to Pleasant Hill. The Civil War Letters of Captain Elijah P. Petty, Walker's Texas Division, CSA.* Norman D. Brown, ed. (Austin, 1982), p. 225.

4. "...it is impossible for language to tell what we had to endure of mental inquietude as well as dread, I tell you nothing but the literal truth. The arrival of the advance of the Yankees alone turned the negroes crazy. They became utterly demoralized at once and everything like subordination and restraint was at an end. All business was suspended and those that did not go on with the army remained at home to do much worse." John H. Ransdell to Gov. Thomas O. Moore, 24 May 1863, *Louisiana Historical Quarterly*, XIV (1931), pp. 491-92.

could manage. A tall, fine-looking man and a gentleman every inch, he looked to be the very man to hush the fears of these ladies. They told him what awful news they had heard. He told them it was true; he had heard it from a reliable source. They gave him a detailed account of their plans, their helplessness, and fears.

Mr. W— placed the tips of his fingers together, displaying his well-kept hands, turned his profound attention to the frightened women as they one after another told of their troubles with sobs. Mrs. Magruder said to him at last, with tears streaming over her face, "Now, Mr. W—, we have decided to ask you to direct us; we don't know what to do. Whatever you advise we will do, and oh, how we thank you for coming to us in this extremity. What do you advise?"

The gentleman arose to his feet to make his wisdom more impressive, and said, "I feel deeply for you ladies, and realize what trouble you are in. Conditions are terrible, and after considering the matter my advise [sic] is, to hope for the best, but to *prepare for the worst*." Thanking them again for their trust in him, he took his departure.

Poor mothers, they mingled their tears, and renewed their promise to stay together, and help each other all they could. They literally took Mr. W—'s advice. [They] stayed on a plantation peopled by a large number of hostile Negroes with no protection but the three dark friends.

We children, nine in number, had been put in the charge of Aunt Margaret. She had immediately hustled us off to the playroom and locked us in. She was expecting [General] Banks to arrive at any minute; she began planning the best way to hide us all. But the flesh was weak; so she hid herself first. She got behind the bed and told us to pile pillows on her. Probably a spirit of mischief was what caused the difficulty; every time the pillows were arranged, one of the older children would say, "But your feet are stickin' out, Aunt Margaret!" In desperation, the old woman finally flung the pillows aside and crawled between the mattresses of the bed. Satisfied at last, she directed us all to get under the bed! What a spectacle we would have presented had a Yankee soldier looked in the door!

We—under the bed—were already prepared for the worst. If we so much as dared giggle, a smothered voice from the bed threatened us with dire punishments. Just after dark, there came a soft tapping just under our window. "Lord Jesus!" came an awful voice from the bed, "Dee's come! You younguns hole yo' breff!"

Then the tapping came again. In the deathlike stillness which followed, we heard a sibilant whisper. Even so, we recognized the voice of Bose. "Aunt Marg'ret!" he was calling softly, "come to de window!"

The trembling old woman crept to the window, and we heard this message: "Mos' Govan done come, and dee's Yankees all over de place. He say tell Miss Becky to come down to do quarter gate an' see 'im a minute. You go tell 'er I'll meet 'er at de back do' an' go wid 'er."

I rolled out from under the bed. Only one thought had gone home—Pere had come! I beat Aunt Margaret to the door. "Whah you gwine?" she asked me sternly.

"To see my Pere!" I almost yelled. Aunt Margaret towered over me in fury. "You git back onder dat bed. Don' you know dat if de whole family goes traipsin' out to see yo' Pa, de Yankees'll ketch 'im sho? En dee'll cut his th'oat from year to year!" The awful gesture with which she accompanied this statement finished me. I rolled back under the bed. Locking us in, Aunt Margaret went to deliver her message.

When I was older, I heard the story of that night. Pere, scouting in the rear of the Confederate army, suddenly found himself caught within the Yankee lines. Being so near home, he trusted to the friendship of Bose to assist him in seeing his family. After a short conference at the entrance to "the quarters," Mere led Pere's horse through the deepest shadow, to the edge of the river. A Negro man there kept a skiff in which he carried occasional passengers across, but he was friendly to the Yankees! There was no time for hesitation, and when he demurred at taking Pere across, Pere quietly drew his pistol and told him to take his choice—go across or go to hell! He went across. Pere's horse swam behind the boat, and when they reached the pine woods on the other shore, this splendid animal carried him swiftly out of danger.

On our side, loyal Bose waited with my anguished mother. They heard no shots ring out, and after a time the colored boy assured her that Mos' Govan was safe, and that she had better go back to the house. He guarded her to the very door.

The Yankees never came that night.

My father was a Confederate soldier. Johnnie and Mamie's father had been one, too, but he had been shot and killed in a battle. Hyson's and Lizzie's father was ready to enlist at the beginning of the war and had died of pneumonia; so we were all ardent rebels. My sister and I were the only ones whose father was in active service, and we were rather looked up to by the other children on this account, Aunt Margaret thought.

Banks' army began at once to make devastating forays up the river and on Bayou Rapides. The families of Confederate soldiers lived in a state of terror and apprehension. Alarming news came of burned homes and all the horrors of an invading enemy.

One day a man driving a pony in a two-wheeled cart came through our neighborhood. He was a Yankee and seemed to be a skillful forager. He was industriously collecting chickens, eggs, and vegetables for the army. He did not offer to buy these supplies. He simply took them. His cart was pretty well loaded, but one of the Negroes told him that there were "just plentys of young chickens up at Dr. Luckett's," just above us. So he went up there and filled his cart to overflowing, and returned driving calmly by, and picking a chicken as he went, the feathers flying in the wind. We all felt mighty mad with him, but there was nothing to be done.

In about an hour, maybe not so long, we heard one of the ladies on the gallery exclaim: "Why what does that mean?" We ran to see, and there was the man with the cart going back up the road. He was bowed over, his head almost on his knees, and on either side of the cart there rode a Confederate soldier, belaboring the unfortunate pony with their "cowhides" (I wonder if you know what a cowhide is? It was a very popular whip.) urging him to a mad gallop. So some of Dick Taylor's men had the "good eats" intended for Banks's men, and besides they had a perfectly good prisoner. We were glad.

We little folks soon became accustomed to the Blue soldiers, and even ventured out into the yard to see the tents set up on the riverbank. The tents, the camp fires, the many soldiers, and the numberless horses entertained us immensely.

An officer stopped one day and spoke to us. He seemed to be kind to the "little rebs," even opened his haversack and gave us a supply of "hard tack" (very dry hard crackers) which we crunched greedily as we were living on corn bread at the time; coffee and flour were unobtainable in our part of the C.S.A.

This officer, I forget his name, took so much interest in the little children who were friendly with him, he stopped to talk with us every day that he rode into the yard and called for the ladies. They answered his call, that is, they came to the front door and he sat on his horse, and the pathetic effort of the ladies to be polite to him seemed to touch him deeply. He asked if the soldiers had given them any trouble? Said he had tried to prevent disturbance at the house but that there were rough characters in all armies. That if they disturbed the family to please report it to him.

Mrs. Magruder told him that the soldiers had not disturbed us, but the presence of the soldiers had demoralized the

Negroes, and they were insolent and refused to obey any order she gave. That they abused the boy Bose, even threatened to kill him because he milked the cow to get milk for her baby just weaned. They had divided the mules and the land and were making a crop for themselves. She wound up this distressing story by asking him to take the Negroes away with him.

Bose was present and was pointed out as the faithful servant. The captain called Bose to him and asked him "where is the cow that gives milk for that baby." Bose meekly replied: "Mary dun turnt her out." "Why didn't you stop her from turning the cow out?" "Dee was all on em mad, an Mary said she was trying ter kill me," was the quiet answer. The captain burst out with a vicious oath, and asked why he did not "take a knife and—disembowel her" or words to that effect.

The captain turned to one of his orderlies and told him to go to the field and the quarter and bring "every d—ned nigger on the place" to him. The plow hands, men and women, bestrode the mules taken from the plows, and came at a gallop with the trace chains jingling, and women and children from the quarter came running to see what great things "dem soldiers" were going to do for them. They rushed up to the officer and looked eagerly at him, expecting only more good news, but dear, dear, dear, such a tirade of abuse fell on their ears as they had never listened to. He told them that if the U. S. army succeeded they, the Negroes, would be free, but until that time they were still slaves, and that they must behave themselves or he would "see about." They were the most crestfallen set I ever saw. They were just stricken with horror.

The officer told them they must be obedient to their mistress and work just as she directed, which they tremblingly promised to do. "Uncle Jim" a tall black Negro had been very sassy and exerted a most unpleasant influence over the other Negroes. Uncle Jim was there and looked as cheap as the others. Mrs. Magruder pointed to him and said, "I wish you would take that man with you, as I cannot manage him." The officer was on horseback. He looked at Uncle Jim and said, "He looks like a mean old devil. I believe I'll cut his head off," drawing a long, glittering sword from his side.

Uncle Jim fell to his knees and begged, "Oh! Master, for Gawd sake spare me." Mrs. Magruder begged for his life, and the friendly Yankee said, "Well, if you say so, I'll let him live." Turning fiercely to the poor frightened Negro: "You strike a trot down the road, and don't you give me any trouble." Poor old Uncle Jim literally galloped down the road, and we saw him no more till after the war was over.

Several days later a Yankee colonel rode up to the gate and inquired for the mistress of the house. When Mrs. Magruder came to the door, he explained that he would like to make his headquarters at the house. He explained that we would be much safer under these circumstances. He said that he could not keep his eyes on the soldiers at all times, and that he did not want any indignities put upon the ladies. At any rate, he was quartered in her home and we children expected vague horrors. We soon learned that this Yankee, at least, was just a human being after all.

One day he opened a gold locket attached to his watch chain, and stated that he would show what was in it to the first little girl who gave him a kiss. I must have descended from Pandora, for I could not stand it. I edged up to him and said I wanted to see. I kissed him, and was given a peep. I saw a miniature of a lovely little girl about my age. When I exclaimed over the locket, the other children gave their kisses and took a look—all but Sister.

"Well!" exclaimed the colonel, "aren't you going to take a look?"

Sister tossed her curls and her eyes flashed. "My Pere told me not to kiss Yankees!" she said.

"Who is your Pere?"

"Govan Williams, Company G, Second Louisiana Cavalry," she rattled off.

The colonel's eyes twinkled. "And don't you ever do it! You stand by what your Pere tells you." A truce had been made, nevertheless. After that we were great friends, and his aides brought us candy and made much of us when they came to report to headquarters. They told us how they wanted to see their children back up North. From then on, we excepted these particular Yankees from our fear and hatred.

Only those who have lived through this period of anguish can understand the intensity of feeling. I was only a little child, but I heard the talk of my elders, and grew resentful over the indignities put upon my people. In later years, I heard many of the stories over and over from my father's lips. There was the one about Ralph Smith's railroad. Ralph Smith was a pioneer in that region and in 1836 he built and operated [one of] the first railroads west of the Mississippi River.[5] It ran from Lecompte to Alexandria, a distance of about twenty miles, and it served to haul the produce of the countryside to a big warehouse on Red River.

When the news of Banks's raid came, Ralph Smith said, "By God, he won't use my railroad!" So he told the engineer to lay tracks to the edge of Red River bluff, then to hook on all the cars and get up steam.

"Now," he said, "run her to the edge of the bluff and let 'er go!" The whole train plunged into the swirling depths of Red River.

During these years, Aunt Mag Texada had many trying experiences.[6] In one of Banks's raids, just as the Yankees were leav-

5. "The 'train' consisted of a locomotive, baggage car and passenger car. When the Yankees destroyed the road they 'laughed until they cried over the 'loco' which was so antique that they had never seen its like." Esther Wright Boyd quoted in Sue Eakin, *Rapides Parish History* (Alexandria, 1976), p. 28.

6. Captain Joseph W. Texada, born 1831, eighth of the eleven children of John A. and Lucy Welsh Texada. In 1852 he married Margaret Davidson.

ing, they set fire to her house. She was all alone. She rushed out on the porch and looked at the retreating men. "Oh my God!" she screamed. Then she called in a clear voice, "Isn't there one *gentleman* in the crowd who will help me save my home?"

A young officer looked back. Calling to several of the men, he rushed back into the house. With the other soldiers bringing water, he soon extinguished the blaze. As long as Aunt Mag lived, she never allowed those charred timbers to be removed.

At China Grove, Aunt Mag's home, you could look right across Bayou Rapides and down Cruikshank Lane. One day a company of Yankees passed. While Aunt Mag was still looking out an upstairs window, she saw a Confederate scout coming up the lane. He stopped, and cautiously peered in all directions. Then he looked toward her window. She waved, then signaled which direction the Federal troop had taken. The soldier galloped back to his company, and they were soon in hot pursuit of the Yankees. A sharp skirmish followed, during which the fight surged backward and forward across the lawn three times. When the firing seemed to have lulled, Aunt Mag persuaded an old negress, Aunt Ruthie, to go with her to carry water to the wounded of both sides. While on their mission of

---

They had two children, J. W. Texada, Jr. and Davidson Ker Texada. His plantation was "China Grove" on Bayou Rapides. From Melrose scrapbook 67, p. 109, Archives Division, NSU: Obituary, Jan. 16, 1926. Mrs. Margaret K. Texada, 90 years old, widow of the late Captain Joseph Texada, died at the residence of her son, Dr. D. K. Texada in Boyce, Friday. Mrs. Texada was born in Alexandria, and was a daughter of the late Dr. Pintard Davidson, who later moved to New Orleans, where he practiced his profession until his death. She is survived by one son, Dr. D. K. Texada, of Boyce; thirteen grandchildren and twenty-one great grandchildren. Funeral service took place Friday afternoon from the family residence in Boyce and to St. Philip's Episcopal chapel. Burial was at McNutt's Hill. *Biographical and Historical Memoirs of Northwest Louisiana* (Nashville and Chicago, 1890), p. 594 (hereafter cited *Northwest Louisiana Memoirs*).

mercy, a Confederate rode up to the gate and begged for a drink. Just as he raised the water to his lips, his horse was shot from under him.

During the same skirmish, Cora Kerr, at her home nearby, took her baby and hid in a gully down the bayou bank. Crouching there, ashen and trembling, she happened to glance across the bayou. On the opposite bank there was another gully, and in it was a Negro woman, with six little black children clutching her. On top of her head was an enormous bundle of clothes. Just then a volley of musketry rattled out. From the other bank came a moan, "Lawd ha' mussy on dis onsartin nigger!"

Seeing herself in the same comical light dispelled Cora's own fear, so she climbed out with her baby and went back to the house.

The same Aunt Ruthie who helped take water to the wounded soldiers was almost as valiant as her white mistress. Returning home one day she found a Yankee soldier prowling about her house. Berating him for a tramp and po'-white-trash, she snatched up a boiler and sailed into him. Not wanting to hurt the old woman, he called to his comrades who had come up to pull her off of him. They shouted with laughter, and said, "Go to it, old woman!" She thrashed him so soundly that finally he ran. Aunt Ruthie rocked with laughter and clapped her hands. "I reckon one Southern done whipped a Yankee!" she exulted.

Before Reconstruction, the Negroes feared and hated the Yankees as much as did the white people of the South.

In 1863 when all our young men were at the battle front engaged in a heroic defense of homes and firesides, there was an outbreak of smallpox in and around the town of Alexandria. It was not possible to fight this terror with vaccination as there was no way to procure vaccine or medicines of any kind on account of the blockade. When the stock of drugs that was in the local drug stores was exhausted there was no base of supply to draw on. The Southern Confederacy was cut off from the world, completely isolated, dependent entirely on the native resources of our sunny land.

When we children had the awful chills and fevers so prevalent at that time, our mothers brewed a nauseous tea made of boneset (a native plant of great bitterness) and willow bark, which was also quite bitter. If you have never partaken of this awful dose, you can form no idea of the superlative nastiness of the decoction. For all our ailments, we had herbs that helped some. For indigestion catnip tea, sage tea, and dittany tea; for colds, "Life Everlasting", a flowering plant from the hills; for sores, bruises and burns there was the soothing jelly made from slippery elm bark soaked in water. For the loathsome disgusting disease smallpox there was nothing.

The malady spread wildly. The country was in a panic. In desperation the few elderly doctors in Alexandria, men too old for the army, decided to inoculate a cow with the scab from a smallpox patient, and create a supply of vaccine.

They vaccinated a fine young milk cow belonging to Dr. French, from a pustule taken from one of their smallpox patients. The cow had a real case of smallpox, and when her sores dried up, they saved the scab, and we were all vaccinated from this cow, and many of our dear soldiers were safeguarded from the same source. Does this seem funny? I think not; it was most pathetic.

Southern women were resourceful! They gathered the native herbs and made remedies for our many illnesses; they parched cornmeal to make their breakfast coffee. The spinning wheels and old wooden looms were brought out. They made beautiful homespun cloth to make clothes for themselves and the many Negroes dependent on them. They made many bright dyes from the plants growing in great profusion in the land. From the black walnut trees, leaves and nuts, they made many shades of brown, and even a deep black. The sassafras made a lovely pink dye.

My mother planted a patch of indigo, and manufactured the beautiful blue so dear to us all. The indigo seeds were sent to her by her sisters in South Carolina (I have a scrap of the "home-spun cloth" of which my aunts made their dresses). They also sent a pleated piece of palmetto, the pattern was called "South Carolina Pleat."

The women wove woolen goods, jeans, to make clothes for their husbands and sons who were in the war. Beautiful and delicate young ladies were expert at the quaint picturesque spinning wheel, keeping time to the musical humming of the wheel by singing the loved war songs: "The Bonnie Blue Flag," "Red, White, and Blue," and one of which I cannot recall the name, but the oft shouted refrain was:

> Fare Ye Well Forever to the Star Spangled Banner,
> No longer shall it wave o'er the land of the free,
> But we will unfold to the broad breeze of heaven,
> Thirteen bright stars round a palmetto tree.

This was a favorite song of Senator J. R. Thornton, a loved friend of my father's; they were both members of Company G, Second Louisiana Cavalry, C.S.A.

This honored and beloved Senator Thornton was a native of Rapides Parish. He attended a meeting of the Louisiana School Men long after the War Between the States. At that meeting he was pointed out as the nearest living relative of George Washington. We thought that the Father of his Country was as much honored by the kinship as our noble senator was.

In 1864 General [Nathaniel] Banks, U.S.A., was making his second raid up Red River in pursuit of General Dick Taylor's

26

army of the C.S.A. My father was one of General Taylor's scouts. He was the last one in the rear of the Confederate army. His business was to find out the number and the probable movements of the troops under General Banks and report same to the Confederate headquarters.

When the Union army took Alexandria my father was quite near the town and was able to gather a good deal of the news of their future plans. He was well acquainted with the country, having lived there before he entered the Confederate army. There was a public road on Bayou Rapides from Alexandria to Cotile landing (now the town of Boyce) where Cotile Bayou flows into Red River, some thirty or more miles above Alexandria.

Bayou Rapides and Bayou Cotile are formed by one or more streams from the pine woods flowing together. Dividing the water they make separate bayous, one flowing northwest and the other southwest. Rapides enters Red River at Alexandria and Cotile flows into the same river fifteen or more miles above.

The roads on either side of these bayous and the one on the river meet at these two towns, leaving a swamp between the river and bayou, not very wide at any point, but a dense swamp, covered by deep morasses, lagoons, and quagmires with bridle paths known only to the residents, going through.

My father lingered near Alexandria to secure some important data and papers for his commander. Seeing a large force of United States soldiers leave Alexandria by the Bayou Rapides road, he struck out in the deep swamp to cross the river road and rejoin his command, then a few miles above Cotile.

Having crossed through the devious paths of the mirey swamp he reached the back lands of the Excelsior plantation (just here is Rapides Station on the T. & P. Railroad). He left his horse hidden and walked into the dilapidated, overgrown fields. The fence rows were covered with a mass of Virginia creeper, brambles, and morning glory vines, tie vines as they were called. This wild growth afforded an excellent hiding place, and he determined to creep under the protecting shadows and see if the way was safe for him to ride on his journey. He had not gone far in the field when he met a Negro boy belonging to Dr. Luckett. He knew the boy, Joe, and tried to disguise his voice, laid his hand carelessly across his face, and asked: "Boy, can you tell me if any one of our men are about here? the Yanks, you know." Joe laughed a low soft gurgle and replied: "Mr. Williams, you can't fool me." Then my father said, "Joe, you will not tell of me, will you?" "Naw Sir," said Joe, "but dem Yanks is all over the place you better look out. I just seed em down de bend road."

Enjoining secrecy on Joe, my father told him where he had left his horse, and then continued his stealthy creeping up the vine-covered fence row. When he was near the river road he saw the enemy coming in great force up the highway. He stooped among the vines and counted the cannons as they lumbered by. He said he was near enough to them to have "touched them with a long fishing pole." Having waited through the long time it took this body of men to pass, crouched among the brambles, he took his way through the well-known fields. Late in the afternoon he walked in the back door of Dr. Luckett's home, to be met with consternation and dismay. The venerable doctor exclaimed: "Oh, Mr. Williams, you cannot stop a minute, the Yankees are all over the place. For God's sake get away before you are captured." My father said: "I will not be taken alive, and I must stop and rest among friends. I am exhausted." Mrs. Luckett said: "Indeed you shall rest, and I will give you a cup of tea." The tea was gratefully received. He told her he would drink if Banks's whole army came just then, that he "had not broken his fast" since the early morning of the past day.

Dear Mrs. Luckett with hospitable haste, prepared a lunch

for him, and as he had fever she gave him a small package of quinine. They all loved him and gave all the sympathy for his terrible plight that words could convey. Joe had been sent for the horse hidden back of the field. Mounting his horse he (father) took a sorrowful leave of his friends, crossed the river to Avoca, the plantation home of Mr. Stephen Mead.

They also were horrified to see him in the Yankee lines. Miss Lilly Mead, Mr. Stephen Mead's niece, begged him to put on a suit of Uncle Stephen's clothes and leave off his Confederate uniform. He told her "no indeed he would not be found in citizens clothes as he would certainly be hanged as a spy if he were." Mr. Mead said, "No, keep on your grey, and don't be taken at all. You can surely get away." My father told him that his horse was broken down and not fit to ride; so Mr. Mead lent him a fresh horse, taking the poor tired horse to care for till better times.

My father rode out in the pine hills on the east side of the river and made his way up to Cotile, to try to rejoin his command at the earliest possible moment. He went to the home of a friend of his, Mr. Boyce, for whom later the town of Boyce took its name. Mr. Boyce and his sister Miss Louise were alarmed when he came in. They told him the last of the Confederates had left there two days before (The Second Louisiana Cavalry, my father's company, were the last to leave), and that the entire country was in the hands of the Federals and advised him to get away as soon as they could give him supper. While the supper was being prepared, the startling news arrived that a party of Federals was coming up the road. My father ran on foot to the river side where a thicket of willows leaned over the water.

The soldiers were galloping up the road in great haste, as my father reached the willow bank, and just there he met a Negro man. He felt sure the man would betray him, but in desperation he asked him "not to tell on him." The man said he would not, and my father asked him the second time not to betray him. The man answered: "You hide, God knows I won't tell." So burning with a fierce fever, sick, tired and heartsore, he sank into the water of the river, clinging to a low hanging branch of a willow tree. Through the fluttering leaves he could see the soldiers when they met the Negro and heard the words, "Hello! hello! did you see the rebel—that was here? We know he was here just a bit ago, and we are going to get him. Did you see him?" "Yas Sir I seed im, when he seed you all comin he run away," the Negro replied.

My father said to himself, "I am lost." The soldiers next asked which way did he go? "Quick tell me." The Negro waved his arm in the opposite direction from the river saying: "he went out to the woods." The fence was knocked down and the men dashed across the fields, and were soon gone. My father managed to cross the river, once more afoot, to look for a safe hiding place in the river swamp. He had one awful chill after another each followed by raging fever. I do not know where he passed the night, in the woods I suppose, and the next morning more dead than alive, he met a gallant boy whom we knew, Rolly Maddox, riding a fresh young horse.

My father told him of his sad plight, and Rolly sprang off his horse and handed the bridle reins to my father. He said: "Here is my horse. He is young and fresh. Take him, and try to save yourself."

Thanking the brave boy and promising to return the horse if possible, my father mounted the fresh steed, and set out on his journey. He managed to elude the enemy soldiers, got across the river once more, and struck off through the green hills to reach Campti, for he heard that his company was there. When he reached Saline swamp he got hopelessly lost, and spent a night in the dark shades of this almost impenetrable forest. When daylight came he found his way out, and was so near the spot where his family were he came home for one day. We were at the Jack Readhimer place near Saline. After one day at home he rejoined his command at or near Campti.

I am glad I can say he returned Rolly's horse unhurt, and he rewarded the two Negroes, Joe and the Boyce Negro, for not betraying him. He taught us always to love Rolly Maddox for the timely aid he gave. He rejoined his command in time to engage in the battles of Mansfield and Pleasant Hill even though he was sick.

When the guns of the battle [Battle of Yellow Bayou, May 18, 1864, near Mansura][7] were hushed, when the surviving men of the war had gone to their several places of rest, and the silent field was covered with the dead and dying men who so short a time since were full of life, hope, and patriotism, the southern sun shone on a woeful sight. Soldiers in blue and gray were dying side by side, victims of one of the wildest scenes of slaughter the sun ever illuminated.

My father, a member of the Second Louisiana Cavalry, had been in the forefront of the bloody fight and in the early morning after the battle, he walked over the battlefield. He said his heart was wrung at sight of the silent friends and foes in the helpless mass very near each other. He lifted the agonized forms and placed them in more comfortable positions, gave water to the thirsty dying men. He was so overcome at the sight of the "poor dumb clay" and the failing voices calling for "water! water!" that "great strong man that he was," he wept aloud, all alone on the field. He saw one Union soldier fatally wounded and twisted tumble as he fell. My father lifted him to

7. The Battle of Yellow Bayou was the last engagement of the Red River Campaign. It occurred on May 18, 1864, south of Alexandria in Avoyelles Parish when Confederate General Richard Taylor tried to block the Union withdrawal to New Orleans. After fierce, often hand-to-hand fighting the Confederates withdrew and the Yankees continued their retreat. Union casualties numbered 267 and the Confederates suffered 500. John D. Winters, *The Civil War in Louisiana* (Baton Rouge, 1963), pp. 376-377.

a more comfortable position, gave him water from his almost empty canteen. The poor fellow soon died, his last moments soothed by a weeping foe.

This foe sat by him till the last fluttering breath was spent. A letter had fallen from the dying man's pocket. My father reverently lifted and read it. It began: "My darling husband," then a loving letter telling him about his little children and how sweet the baby was, how she loved him and longed for his return. My father said it was heartbreaking to find this sweet, loving message in such a scene of carnage.

He was instrumental in having this man buried in a spot that he could in some future day identify. Then he enclosed the letter from the dead soldier's pocket to the address given by the writer and told her of his finding it, of the burial of her husband, and promised to direct her to the spot if she should ever come to this place. The mails were uncertain at that time, and perhaps she did not receive it. We have never heard from her.

Fifty years after this bloody battle I visited this historic spot. Large trees had grown up, and leaping vines were growing there. Wild flowers flourished and bloomed in colorful abandon where once so many lives were lost. In several places near the fort there were luscious waxy leaves of some tender plant, blood red in color, thrusting their gory leaves up among the soft green of the many ferns waving gently in the breeze. Of course, this is perfectly natural, but I could not repress a thrill of horror at the thought that these little plants were still gathering the "ruddy drops" shed so ruthlessly half a century ago. Many years have passed since the battle of Yellow Bayou. The men in gray and the men in blue who survived are nearly all gone to "that land from whose shore no traveler returns." The ranks of the two armies are so thinned that soon they will have their reunions together. The war between the States will soon be a romantic, heroic story, and the glory of each side will be claimed by all. Let us forget the enmity and try to remember that our sometime foes "are brothers; they are men."

While we old folks love with passionate devotion "the flag that once challenged the gaze of the world" we will have to submit to having our children and children's children march beneath the Stars and Stripes, and sing the battle songs that once were like poison to our souls.

III

The War Continues

We had been back on the river about a year and a half when Pere came in unexpectedly one day. As soon as greetings were over, he told Mere that they were expecting Banks to make another raid any time, and that he had obtained a three-day leave to move us to a safer place. Where safer than our beloved sand hills, where we had so many dear friends? Never was there such hurrying and scurrying. We children were wild with excitement, and poor Mere had little sympathy from us in this new trial. A strong team was hitched to a big wagon, and we carried with us only what it would contain. No time could be lost.

Just as we were ready to depart, our joy was suddenly quenched. Tom Green leaped on the porch, tail waving. "Oh, we forgot Tom Green!" I cried, and began climbing out to get him. Pere and Mere exchanged glances, and Mere caught my skirt. She then explained that a special box would have to be made in which to carry him, and there was not time for that. Sister and I at once began wailing lustily. "The other children will take care of him for you till we come back," comforted Mere. The wagon began to move.

"Cora, don't forget to scratch behind his ears!" I sobbed.

Even such sorrow as ours was soon forgotten on the wonderful trip back to the hills of Natchitoches Parish. To this day, when I enter the moving stillness of a longleaf pine forest, I am back again on a loaded wagon, creaking up a long sand hill, dipping down into delicious hollows. I can see golden water rippling over pebbles, the wet white sand quivering with yellow butterflies. I can smell the sweet-myrtle sprays which the driver broke and stuck in the horses' bridles to keep the flies away.

We were nearing the end of our journey. I had drifted off to sleep when suddenly I was electrified by an announcement from Pere. "This is Choctaw Creek; we are nearly to the Pattersons'," he said. No more sleep for me! I was going to see my long-lost playmates again! It seemed to me that the wagon wheels almost ceased to turn, we moved so slowly.

We got there at last, and at Pere's "Hello," they all came out. When the children recognized us, they swarmed over the wagon. What joyful greetings! Questions flew so fast it was impossible to answer them all. We could stop only a few minutes, as it was getting late, but when the children learned that Mere, Sister, and I had actually come to stay, they consented to let us go.

Pere had engaged board for us with our old friend, Mrs. Readhimer, and we reached there just at dusk. She gave us a warm welcome and a good supper, and we fell into bed. At daylight the next morning, Pere kissed us goodbye and went back to the army.

Mere must have felt desolate, but Sister and I soon forgot our sorrow in refinding old friends and making new ones. The very first day after we returned, our nearest neighbors came to see us. They were the children and grandchildren of Dr. Sweat, who had moved from South Carolina during our brief sojourn on the river.[1] The callers included six little girls! In a short

1. Benjamin Screven Sweat died October 28, 1878, and Mrs. Sweat died September 8, 1889. "The Big House is gone now and the huge oaks that stood in the front yard are slowly dying of old age. Only the road that runs east and west is still exactly as it was when my mother and her playmates ran over it during the War, except for the changes Nature has made. There were Sallie, Screven, Carrie, and Betty Sweat, Gena, Alice, Hattie, and Clarence Edgerton, Mary and Dosia Williams (friends whose mother was a refugee from the War area), and a retinue of little Negroes. They were all too young to be greatly

while our first shyness wore off, and then what fun we had! The children were cousins of the Pattersons and usually the whole crowd played together.

Everything was perfect until Mr. Loe [of Bienville Parish] came courting Mrs. Readhimer, who was a widow. Her handsome sons were away in the army, and probably she was lonely. At any rate, she married Mr. Loe, and left us.[2] Mere was equal to the occasion. She rented the place from Mrs. Loe, rented a pony, and hired a slave, June, from one of the neighbors. Then she put in a crop! She bought a brood sow, and by fall she had a drove of shoats, and corn to feed them on. So, in a time of much suffering, we had food.

When [the new] Mrs. Loe left us, another difficulty presented itself. She took all her household goods with her. When we had fled from the river, it was impossible to bring anything except necessities. We had planned to board, so had no need of such things as kitchenware. It was impossible to buy anything of the sort. Now our neighbors proved the real meaning of the word—each contributed one or two needed articles: a cup and saucer, a dishpan, two or three plates, or a knife, fork, and spoon. It was a remarkably varied assortment, but it served our purpose. In the hard days of the war, the women and old men who were left at home practiced real communism, each dividing his sparse store of food or other necessities with those around him as long as there was one thing left. Now we were established at housekeeping and farming, and began to have a feeling of permanency.

There was no school in the neighborhood; so Mrs. Patterson

---

affected by the War." Virginia Trotti Dormon Miller, "Ancestors and Descendants of Gaspar Joseph Trotti," Pinckard Collection, NSU.

2. Note from Stephen P. Loe family Bible: "Stephen P. Loe and Harriet Readheimer was married January 31st, 1864." Eva Loe McDuffie Collection, NSU.

taught her own and Dr. Sweat's children. For friendship's sake, she consented to take Sister and me, too. Whether or not I learned anything I cannot say, for I remember little of lessons. Far clearer in my mind are the trips to and from school. We had to cross the Eight-mile, a small pinewoods creek. What child of flesh-and-blood could resist stopping to wade in amber water, rippling over firm sand?

A still smaller stream, a mere rill, ran into the Eight-mile just where it crossed the road. It trickled down a shallow ditch by the roadside for some distance, and one afternoon I was inspired to make a dam across it. In a little while I had quite a pool of water collected. Nettie always seemed to admire my enterprise, so she set to work and made her a dam, too. It never occurred to me to make a runway around my tiny levee; so Nettie, below me, got no water. She complained, but I said I couldn't help it, and that I had made mine first. The argument grew warmer, and suddenly Nettie swooped down and made a break right in the middle of my dam. Well, immediately there was war right at home! I slapped Nettie, and she slapped back. Then her sister, my adored Hattie, took sides against me, and that was my last straw. I became a wildcat, and scratched and pulled hair indiscriminately. Screven, who was older, tried to shame us, but he might as well have talked to a whirlwind. Sister, always the perfect lady, did not offer to help me out! Neither did the other older girls. They joined in the verbal quarrel, and after the actual fight was over, bitter words were exchanged until the parting of the way separated us.

My lip was cut, and Sister shudderingly wiped away the blood. When we reached home, we poured out our side of the fray; I expecting sympathy. As a final crushing blow, Mere said she was so mortified she didn't know what to do, and that I would have to apologize to Nettie! Before she could get us bathed and dressed—I was an unholy sight—here came Mrs. Edgerton, Nettie and Hattie's mother, and her two sisters, our beloved Miss Fannie and Miss Jennie.[3] Behind them, with hanging heads, came the other two combatants. Bringing up the rear, the other children came, filled with curiosity to see the outcome of the affair.

"Oh," said Mere, "I was just getting Dosia ready to go over to

3. Obituary of Virginia S. Sweat: Virginia S. Sweat was born in Barnwell County, S.C., February 17, 1844; died November 8, 1902, at the residence of her sister Mrs. L. W. Stephens. Frances Coroneos, born November 13, 1841, died December 29, 1914, buried at Old Saline Church. Ann Trotti Sweat, daughter of Mr. and Mrs. B. S. Sweat, born 24 October 1832, Barnwell District, died 24 November 1888, Saline, La. She married Dr. Edwin Tracy Edgerton on September 19, 1851, at Briarwood Plantation, on the Edisto River, Barnwell County, S.C. He enlisted in the Confederate army. Dormon Collection, NSU. Poem composed by Dr. Edgerton in the Spring of 1888 while lost in the woods of Winn Parish one rainy night:

I can't imagine where I am.
But there's one thing I know,
I'm in Winn Parish badly lost,
And don't know where to go.

The night is very dark and rainy,
And I am cold and wet,
But I can stand it till daylight,
So there's no use to fret.

When morning comes I'll find some place
Where I have often been,
And then I'll travel right away,
From the free state of Winn.

If I could only get a call
To visit some poor devil,
I'd thank the man who made the call
And think his head was level.

But there's no call for me tonight;
I'll have to tough it out.
No man on earth could follow me
Along my crooked route.

your house and apologize for her outrageous behavior. I was never. . . ."

Mrs. Edgerton could not wait for her to finish. "Why," she broke in, "I was never so ashamed of my children! There were two of them fighting poor little Dosia! Anyhow, Nettie had no business to break her dam." Then I said I was sorry, and Nettie and Hattie said they were, too, and the war was over. In a few minutes we were all playing together as gayly as ever.

The Sweat and Edgerton children were in the habit of having

I'm not as happy as most men
But happier far than some,
And yet I'd give a whole month's practice
To see daylight come.

For there's no call for me tonight,
No rest from my day's ride,
No friendly voice to greet my ear,
And me from these woods guide.

I hear the screech owl's doleful scream
And a cowbell far away,
But the whip-poor-will's sweet melody
Tells me it's almost day.

Daylight will be here in another half an hour,
And I will depart with joy,
In the meantime a doggerel mind
I will employ.

While sitting on my hungry horse,
Making up this rhyme,
I guess my friend Joe Harper
Thinks I failed to come on time.

But if the gnats don't eat me up
I'll get there by and by
And then I'll tell him why I failed
Although I was so nigh.

their hair "shingled"[4] early in the summer. This summer we joined them. It was quite a ceremony. The shingling took place at Dr. Sweat's and, immediately afterward, we repaired to the Eight-mile for our first swim of the season. We were splashing about—eight little girls—in our favorite "hole," which was right by the road. We saw two men coming on horseback. "Duck, quick!" said someone, so we ducked. As the men came up, one of them called, "Howdy boys! Havin' a good time?" We never questioned that he really thought we were boys, and our joy in the great day was complete.

But when daylight comes
I bid farewell, ye lonely hills,
In one more hour I'll be there,
Making up more pills.

While marching through this wilderness
Returning from my camp,
I feel as though I looked
Just like an ordinary tramp.

But what is this I see ahead!
A road I've often traveled,
And since the morning light has come
The mystery is unraveled.

For yonder is Joe Harper's house,
And the cowbell I heard last night,
And there stands his big spotted dog
Most anxious for a bite.

After staying in the woods last night
Wandering all around,
With my hymn-book poet I can say
"I once was lost but now
                    I'm found."
Virginia Miller typescript, Pinckard Collection, NSU.

4. Shingled hair was trimmed short from the back of the head to the nape.

The lovely summer days went by—filled with fishing, swimming, watermelons, and happy play with little Negroes. Soon muscadines were ripening, and sloes, and these matters required our attention. As I said, school troubled us but little. Later, there were chinquepins and hickory nuts to be gathered.

Carrie, my favorite of the Sweat children, had had two pet cats to go wild. This had distressed her very much, and we had talked about it among ourselves. To my intense delight, they began coming to our house at night, after we had gone to bed. They were afraid of us, but had made friends with our big gray cat, Bob. When I told her about it, Carrie could not wait to come to our house and see her lost pets. Of course all the other children wanted to come, too. After Mere gave an urgent invitation, their parents consented for them all to come spend the night.

What a thrilling experience! Mere placed mattresses down on the floor, so it was as if we all slept in one big bed. As soon as supper was over, we went to bed, and tried to get quiet, so the cats would come. Our cat, old Bob, was dozing by the fire. Finally, the whispering and giggling ceased, and Bob decided we were asleep. A small square hole had been cut in the wall to allow the cat to come and go. Bob walked to this, put his head out, and gave a peculiar mew. There was a faint answer from outside. Bob came back, and presently a white head appeared at the hole. This was Whitey, one of Carrie's cats! Probably the strain was too much for her, and she gasped and moved. At any rate, the white head disappeared. Bob went to the hole again and reassured him, and in a few minutes he slipped into the room. Right behind him crept Jim, the other cat. Then all three friends settled down by the fireplace for a warm nap! Firelight flickering on the ceiling was soothing, and, in spite of our excitement, we, too, were soon fast asleep.

Children must play, regardless of breaking hearts. Christmas during the war must have been a mockery to the older people, but my memory of the time is not marred by one stab of pain. We knew that Santa Claus would come, regardless of conditions, but we were somehow made to understand that his gifts would be suited to the time. How our mothers must have schemed and planned and consulted together!

We were up at the peep of day to look at our stockings. Mere could scarcely keep us in the bed until June finished building a roaring fire of pine-knots and oak logs. There, in the top of each stocking was a doll!—and such a doll—made of rags, stuffed with cotton, and dressed in scraps of gay calico, but beautiful in our eyes. I do not attempt to explain why children were not critical in those days. There were gingercakes, cut in wonderful shapes of bird and beast. There were popcorn-balls, made with molasses—oh, delicious!

Just as soon as we had finished looking at our own things, we were wild to be off to see what Santa Claus had brought the Sweat and Edgerton children—never stopping to reason that it would, of necessity, be much the same as our own. As soon as it was broad daylight, Mere let us go. We went into new ecstasies over *their* rag dolls, peanut and popcorn candy, and gingercakes. There could be no other kind of cake, as sugar was unobtainable.

There was only one variation in the gifts. In ransacking trunks and chests for available materials, Miss Fannie had unearthed two little china dolls' heads. Rag bodies were made for them, and they were duly dressed. So Carrie's and Betty's dolls were wonderful, indeed. As Carrie was my particular chum, I played with her doll the most, and remember distinctly how beautiful it was. The whole doll was not over eight inches long, but it was dressed complete, with ruffled petticoat and panties. Her dress was of bright yellow calico, sprigged with tiny red flowers.

Next came the round of the "quarters." All of us, about a dozen children, had to visit each cabin, slip up and yell

"Christmas Gift!" We then showed our dolls, and divided our candy and cakes with any of the children who had none of their own. Now when I see our modern children, bored in an hour with their expensive toy automobiles and aeroplanes, I think of those long-ago Christmases—and pity the poor little overpampered things of today.

Another joyous occasion was my eighth birthday. Mere invited all the children to spend the day with me! I do not remember what we had for dinner, but certainly there was no fine birthday cake with candles. What I do remember is how all the children deferred to me, because it way my birthday. This was most unusual, as I was the youngest! They must do something special in my honor; so at last they decided they would make a swing. They quietly appropriated Mere's calf-rope, and tied it between two blackjack saplings. Then each took turn swinging me, running-under, and sending me as high as possible. I had never felt so honored! For that day, at least, I was queen.

In those days, there was a mutual respect between children and elders that was sweet and gracious. I remember once when Miss Fannie and Miss Jenny came out to see us at our play-house under the big oaks at Dr. Sweat's. They were all serious-ness. We had a glass bottle which we called a telescope. Miss Jenny picked it up and looked through it, heavenward. She said that was wonderful, that she had always wanted to look through a telescope. Then Miss Fannie sat down and played the piano—a big oak stump! She said it had such a sweet tone! That grown-up young ladies, who could play on real pianos, and who had beaus, should so honor us was thrilling indeed.

My memory of my mother at this time is always associated with the swing and bump of the loom. One of the most remarkable things of all time is the amount of work accomplished during the Civil War by gently bred women, accustomed since babyhood to being waited on "hand-and-foot." My mother spun and wove nine hundred yards of cloth! Many of the slaves were

44

kept busy spinning and weaving, but the white women had to take a hand, too; for, in addition to the home needs, the soldiers had to be supplied with uniforms. I wish I were an artist, that I might paint a portrait of my mother at the loom, in her splendid young strength and grace, moving the treadle, throwing the shuttle.

It was a time that called forth ingenuity. Very old women searched their memories for names of roots and herbs of which dyes could be made. For the first time since pioneer days, there was much searching, digging, and drying. From the sweet-leaf was made a bright yellow, and sassafras produced a delicate pink. From black walnut was obtained a rich brown. Blue was not satisfactory. It was made from wild false indigo, and was dull, with a purplish tinge. Mere loved blue, and determined to have it—the right shade; so she wrote to South Carolina for real indigo seed.

Nothing was ever cared for more tenderly than this crop of indigo, and, strange to say, it prospered. When it was just the right stage, the green stalks were cut and packed into barrels. Water was then poured over, and it was left to soak until it became quite soft. With a hoe for a dasher, this was churned to a pulpy mass. The fiber was then removed, leaving a thick, blue liquid. This was allowed to settle for several days, when the water was carefully drained off. When all moisture had evaporated, there was a thick cake of sediment in the bottom of the barrel. This was the precious blue dye for which we had longed. Of course Mere divided with our dear neighbors.

I well remember a dress that Sally Sweat had at this time.[5] Sally was a darling, and all of us, young and old, loved to do things for her. She was so young and gay, I suppose her older

5. Sarah Maria Means Sweat, born 22 March 1849, Barnwell District, S.C., died Coushatta, 26 January 1909. She married Leonard Waller Stephens at Sparta, La., in January 1869. Virginia Miller manuscript, Pinckard Collection, NSU.

sisters hated for her never to have anything to wear except the usual subdued colors of our homespun; so Miss Jenny introduced an innovation. She found an old piece of a red silk sash and frayed it out into a soft down. As the piece of cloth was being woven, someone stood by and now and then thrust in a bit of this bright fluff. The finished cloth was a perfect success—the dark brown ground gayly flecked with red. How Sally loved that dress, and how we all loved her in it!

This makes me think of another incident in which Sally figured prominently. She was Mere's favorite of the girls. She always seemed to know just when Mere needed cheering up. If there had been a battle at the front, and no one knew which son, father, or brother might have been killed, Sally always appeared to make my mother forget the awful hours—perhaps days—of suspense. I can see her yet as she came swinging up to the gate, slender, graceful, quivering with life. Before she reached the gate she would give a whoop, wave her nightgown over her head, and announce that she had come to spend the night.

One time she said that Dr. Sweat had sent her over to learn to spin. "Sis Jenny and Sis Fannie and all the rest have given me up as hopeless," she laughed. "Pere said if you could teach me to weave a piece of homespun fit to make Maum Silvy a cook apron, he'd be thankful!" Mere fell right into the trap—I know that it was no less—and for two days we kept busy and laughing, teaching this clever, droll girl how to warp and size, how to treadle and turn the beam. Dear Sally! She was wise enough to know when to appear awkward.

After the war had been over for several months, news spread over the neighborhood that Turner's store had received a shipment of goods of all sorts.[6] Mere was eager to go and find out if

6. During the Civil War Turner's Store in Saline stood where there is a service station now, in the northeast part of Saline. It was an old building, high off the ground. Ladies rolled bandages there during the Civil War. Later

she could get some dishes. She asked her favorite girl to go with her. Sally was even more eager than she, for the girls were all excitement over the new dress goods that had arrived, and no wonder, poor young things, for it had been long since they had *bought* cloth for dresses. Her father had consented for her to have a dress. As she was to make several small purchases for the family, also, he gave her his purse, with every cent of cash on hand at the time. It contained forty dollars.

[When we] arrived at the store, it turned out that gossip had not done justice to the truth. Turner did indeed have a surprising showing of dress goods, rich, soft silks in several bright shades. It was too much for a beauty-loving young girl, who for four years had dressed in homespun. Discretion flew to the winds—she forgot self-denial, the hard schooling of war. Mere was indulging in the wild extravagance of calico and "store-bought" stockings for Sister and me. When she rejoined Sally, what was her astonishment to find the clerk folding length after length of silk! "And what is that?" she asked.

"I've bought me a dress," Sally exulted, "and oh, isn't it pretty!" She still had not come down to earth. Mere was speechless. She had priced some of the silks.

When Sally paid for her purchases, Mere could see that she emptied her purse. It was too late to do anything about it, anyhow, and she could not bear to dash the child's high happiness. There was not much conversation as they drove home. Mere was miserable, but she had no idea how she could help the situation. At least she could stand by her favorite, and lend her moral support; so she got out with her when they reached Dr. Sweat's. Still bewitched, Sally bounded out of the buggy and rushed in the house to show her purchase.

"Everybody shut your eyes!" she said. Then she spread the

Webby Driggers owned the place. Conversation with Gladys Britt, 1984, Saline, La.

goods out on the bed—ten yards of bright blue silk grenadine! "Now look!" and she danced about on tiptoe, waiting for their admiration.

There was a dead silence. Everybody looked, and Sally looked at them. Gradually her sensitive face changed. "Why-why-what's the matter?" she stammered.

Her father cleared his throat, then said gently, "How much did the dress cost, daughter?"

"Four dollars a yard. . . ." She hesitated. She was beginning her descent from the clouds.

"Did you get Sis Jenny's shoes?" This was Miss Fanny.

A look of fright crept into the child's eyes. "I forgot them!" she gasped. Her mouth quivered.

"Did you get the teacups, Honey?" asked her mother.

"I-I-forgot them, too!" This was a wail.

Here Mere stepped in and tried to help her favorite out. She said it was her fault, that Sally was so young she should have known to help her with her purchases. Dr. Sweat would not have it.

"No," he said, "Sally must learn responsibility. She knows how scarce money is, and she should not have thought only of herself at a time like this. She. . . ." but he got no further, for Sally threw herself into his lap, her arms around his neck.

"Oh, Pere!" she sobbed, "I'm so sorry! I will take the dress back. I'll get somebody else to buy it. I forgot we didn't have any money for pretty things!"

He told her that she had bought the dress, and she must keep it. "Always stand by a trade," he said. "And none of our neighbors can afford luxuries any more than we can. No, you will make the dress and wear it, and look as pretty as you can. We will manage somehow to get the things we need. It will soon be time to sell the cotton, and then I will get Fanny and Jenny each a dress and some shoes." Finally he laughed and patted her head. "You will forget it all by the time you are married twice!"

Soon Sally had need for the new dress, for she was going on a visit to Sparta. This was a gay little place in those days, the seat of Bienville Parish, and quite a center of culture. Soon, all hands, that is, the women and girls, were working on the famous dress, and the sorrow connected with its purchase was forgotten. Then arose the question of Sally's hair. She had been crowned with glory to only a limited degree, her hair being soft and fine as silk, and not overly abundant. Alas, the style of the moment called for a coronet braid wound about the head! Sally was in despair. She felt sure the effect of the wonderful dress would be entirely lost if set off by nothing more impressive than her demurely sleek little head.

Once more Mere came to the rescue. By a strange coincidence, her hair and Sally's were the same shade of soft brown. Mere had more hair than she knew what to do with—it hung to her knees. So she slipped into another room and got one of the older girls to clip out a strand here and there where it would not show. It did not take many snips of the scissors to supply abundant material for her purpose. She fastened the ends of the hair together, and plaited it smoothly; with her hand behind her, she went back into the room.

"Shut your eyes and sit still," she told Sally. Then she pinned the braid around her head. When the surprised girl opened her eyes and dashed to a mirror, she was in ecstasy. She hugged Mere; she danced; she laughed; she cried. Life was perfect, and in a few days she advanced in triumph on the unsuspecting town of Sparta.

IV

After The War

One of the strangest things about life is how certain scenes stand clear, all bridging incidents left out. One sweet spring day, I was playing under the big oaks at Carrie and Bettie's house.[1] Some soldiers came straggling up to the gate. They called "Hello!" and Dr. Sweat came out. A man wearing an officer's cap spoke. He said only three words.

"Lee has surrendered!"

Dr. Sweat's face got white, and he leaned on his cane, staring at the man.

"My God!" he said. Then he turned and walked slowly into the house. We had never noticed before that he was a very old man.

Everybody acted strangely. We children thought people ought to be happy because the war was over and all the men would come home soon. Instead, their faces were set and grey, and

---

1. Caroline Trotti Sweat, born 12 March 1853, Barnwell, S.C., died at Arcadia, La., April 10, 1907. Catherine Elizabeth Sweat, born 29 October 1854, Barnwell District, S.C., died near Colfax, La., 23 February 1931. Dr. Benjamin Screven Sweat of Briarwood Plantation in the northern part of Natchitoches Parish was a scholarly gentleman whose ancestors came to America from the German states in 1699, settling on the coast of South Carolina, and afterwards taking a prominent part in the building of Savannah, Ga. Dr. Sweat was both a minister and a physician. He was one of the early pastors of Old Saline Church, one of the oldest Baptist churches in the state. Dr. Sweat's wife was the granddaughter of Captain Gasper Joseph Trotti, a Revolutionary soldier. Virginia Trotti Dorman Miller, typescript, Pinckard Collection, NSU.

nobody laughed at anything. It was like when someone was very sick in the house.

Then Pere came home. He looked as if he would never laugh again. He couldn't stay in one place but a little while. He and my mother talked in the night. Sometimes we heard them. So many times we heard Mere say, "We can start all over again." Pere would say, "Where?"

After while they began talking about going back to the river. Pere made several trips to look around. It was winter again before we actually went. The whole country was suffering a sort of paralysis, and things moved slowly. The Yankees had carried off or destroyed every vehicle, and my father could find nothing in which we could make the journey. Finally, our beloved godmother, the elder Mrs. Luckett, lent her family carriage. Never shall I forget the grandeur of that return. The carriage still retained some of its ancient richness, and Sister and I could not have been more delighted with Cinderella's own coach. There were silver handles on the doors, glass windows that could be raised and lowered by velvet straps, and steps that could be let down and taken up. Pere was sick, so Mere took the driver's seat on the outside, high in front, and gathered up the reins. On the "boot" behind was placed one trunk, which held everything we were allowed to carry with us! We had slipped our precious storybooks in the bottom of the carriage, and there they lay in a pile for everyone to stumble over. Finally, in exasperation, Pere threw them out. Our anguish was soon lost in the delight of the trip. The old coach swayed over the country roads, and we were great ladies going abroad.

Toward night, we stopped and made camp in the pinewoods in Winn Parish. Just as our fire began to burn brightly, a wagon drove up and stopped by "our" little stream.

"Hello there!" called a man's voice.

"Hello yourself!" answered Pere.

"Well, where've you been and where are you going?" asked the stranger.

"If you want to know, I'm just back from hell," said Pere, "and I'm going to do the best I can."

"Same with me!" came the answer. "Do you mind if we camp here, too?"

"Looks like there's plenty of room for us all," Pere replied. Soon another fire was burning, and the smell of frying bacon began to mingle with the sweetness of the pines. Sister and I made friends with the children of the party. After supper the grown people drifted over, and we all sat around the fire and talked together. Later we sang war songs: "Wait for the Wagon," "Bonnie Blue Flag," "Nettie Moore," and many others . . . but not "Dixie" . . . that was too close to our hearts.

The next night we reached Cotile Landing, on Red River.[2] The next, we came to Ashbourne, where we were to live.[3] This was the plantation belonging to our old friends, the Lucketts. Sugar

2. Cotile community is located in the northwest sector of Rapides Parish, about four miles southwest of Red River. Water transportation provided a connection to Alexandria via Bayou Rapides. A stage road traveled a route of its own along Bayou Rapides to Cotile, thence northward to Monette Ferry, Isle Brevelle, and Natchitoches. Patsy K. Barber, *Historic Cotile* (n.p., 1967), p. 7.

3. "Ashbourne, on Red River near what is now Rapides Station on the T. & P. R. R., was the property of Dr. Levin Luckett who married Miss Adaline Crain, a daughter of Col. Crain. There were born of this union two sons and six daughters. Dr. Robert Levin Luckett, and Henry Payton Luckett; the daughters were Elixabeth, Frances, Ellen, Delia, Ada, and Cora. Dr. Robert L. Luckett volunteered for service in the Confederate army at the beginning of the war [and] served on the battlefields of Virginia all through the terrible struggle. Henry, the second son, was a youth of tender age at the beginning, but while still in his 'teens' he also enlisted in the Confederate service. Ashbourne was the first home in Rapides Parish to hoist the Bonnie Blue Flag. The family were all ardent Rebels, and Confederate soldiers were joyfully entertained by the beautiful and fascinating Luckett girls. On one occasion a party of tired, hungry soldiers came in just as the family was sitting down to dinner. The young ladies arose hastily, invited the men in to dinner, and stood about the table and served the soldiers with their own fair hands. Mrs. Luckett's flower garden was famed far & wide as the most beautiful collection of rare roses and other flowers to be seen in many miles." Dosia Moore, Melrose Collection, NSU.

mill, gin, and fences had been burned during Banks's raids, but Ashbourne was still beautiful, even in its ruins. The old garden was still there, and the trees. The great gardenia bushes had a neglected look, but they were starred with their fragrant white blossoms. Careless cavalrymen had broken the fine old japonicas, but their leaves still glistened bright green.

The next morning after our return, the Luckett children came, lugging an enormous yellow cat. Could *that* be Tom Green? As if to prove his identity, he walked over to the champagne basket which had formerly been his bed, sniffed it, then climbed in and curled up.

There being no school, the elder Mrs. Luckett taught her nephews, the younger Blanchard boys. To Mere's joy, she offered to teach us, too. Those school days with our beloved teacher are quite vivid in my mind. She taught us, the five children, in her own room. The regular school room, in the yard, was occupied by the tutor and the older boys. I remember when Newton and I began grammar, we studied from the same book, and there was much rivalry between us.[4]

In the dull monotony of life immediately after the close of the war, small incidents stand out clearly. One day a soldier in the Federal uniform galloped by during a pouring rain. By his side rode his wife and a mulatto woman. They were all laughing and chatting together! I heard the scandalized comments of my elders. I also remember that they said the man was General George Custer.[5] We children admired the shining rain coats worn by Mrs. Custer and Eliza. They were laughing and gay in

4. "Roselawn, near Boyce, was the home of Mr. Carey Blanchard, father of Mr. Newton Blanchard who was at one time the honored and much loved governor (1904-1908) of Louisiana. Dosia Moore, Melrose Collection, NSU.

5. General George Armstrong Custer married in 1864 Elizabeth, daughter of Judge Daniel S. Bacon of Monroe, Michigan. Allen Johnson and Dumas Malone, eds., *Dictionary of American Biography* (New York, 1930), V, 7. Elizabeth B. Custer wrote of her stay in Alexandria: "We sometimes rode for miles along the country roads, between hedges of osage-orange on one side,

spite of the rain and their hostile surroundings. I am glad to remember the lighthearted laughter, and to know she was happy then, before the awful news of "Custer's last stand" shocked the whole country. Pleasure and pain are closely allied on this sorrowful earth.

There were almost incessant rains in the early spring and summer of 1866. The annual "spring rise" filled Red River and the continual rain added to the full river caused a terrible over-flow in June of that year.[6] Water was five feet deep at our front steps. The river was covered with wrecked houses, pieces of lumber, and many things to attract the attention of two little girls, my sister and myself. One day a chicken coop floated down with a large rooster perched on top. He was alive and very much alarmed by the angry water lashing at his feet. We always hoped that his coop touched land somewhere, and that he fluttered to safety. We children soon learned to guide a small raft about the yard, and then growing braver, we ventured out in the wide lawn.

Water covered the whole country lying between the pine woods on either side of the river for a long month. One day a poor dog came swimming down, howling at every kick. We called to him but he turned, going from the river, and if his strength held out he reached the land. We never knew his fate.

---

and a double white rose on the other, growing fifteen feet high. The dew enhanced the fragrance, and a lavish profusion was displayed by nature in that valley, which was a constant delight to us." Elizabeth B. Custer, *Tenting on the Plains* (New York, 1887), p. 82.

6. "More than a million acres were planted in cotton in Louisiana in 1866, but only some 131,000 bales were harvested. . . . Fed by heavy rains and checked by the swollen Mississippi, the Red River at the end of May flooded its narrow valley from Indian Territory (Oklahoma) down to its mouth. Alexandria was reported to be under three to six feet of water. . . . Thousands of people, black and white, were left destitute. . . ." Joe Gray Taylor, *Louisiana Reconstructed 1865-1877* (Baton Rouge, 1974), p. 344.

In the spring before the overflow General Custer was stationed at Alexandria. He and his staff occupied the home of Dr. John Casson, on 7th and Jackson Street where the Emanuel Baptist Church now stands.

Sometimes innocent happenings took on significance. There was in the neighborhood a Biloxi Indian by the name of Turn Going. He had been a Confederate soldier, and was liked and respected by everyone. Recently a man whom we will call Jones had come down from the North, bought a nearby plantation, and set himself up in great style. Whether or not he flaunted his prosperity in the faces of his impoverished neighbors I do not know, but he was not very popular with them.

One day several old soldiers were lounging about in the lobby of the Ice-house Hotel when Mr. Jones walked in. With quite an air he lighted a big cigar, bought a paper, then sat down to take his ease. Turn Going was there, and, looking at one of his white friends, he said, "Who is that?"

On some impish impulse the man addressed said, "Why, that's a damn Yankee, Turn! Throw your coat over his head!"

Without a moment's hesitation the old Indian slipped off his long ragged coat, walked up behind Mr. Jones, and simply wrapped him up. There he held him. Turning to his friends, he asked blandly, "What must I do with him?"

Mr. Jones was emitting muffled yells, "Murder! murder!" Smothering their laughter, the men released him and apologized, explaining that it was just a joke. Mr. Jones was convinced that someone had sinister designs on him, and left on the next train. Evidently he made a great story of it, for a Northern paper carried an exciting tale of the "outrage." He wrote back to a lawyer, placing his business in his hands. He sold his plantation and never returned.

The famous Ice-house Hotel received its name from the fact that ice was kept there during the summer. It was cut on northern lakes in winter, shipped on the train, and stored in big cellars.

The first year on the river passed quickly, and Pere announced that he had rented the General Long Place, on Bayou Rapides. We were quite excited and pleased at the prospect of living at lovely old Elgeeton.[7] The gardens had been famous for their beauty and the rare plants they contained, but since the neglected years during the war, enemy weeds had crept in. No longer were flowers kept in the bounds of prim beds, but wandered at will. Ragged robins, the gay vagabonds, slipped in among the perennial phlox and peonies. Verbena, larkspur, and love-in-a-mist foregathered in every sunny spot. In February, the landscape gleamed with golden jonquils.

Gradually we had been picking up the dropped threads of our lives. Old friendships were renewed, and were sweeter than ever. Five of our dearest friends, Kate, Lulie, Bettie, Mattie, and Willie Texada, lived on the next plantation up the bayou, and we were constantly together.[8] Bloomfield, the home of dear Delia Dawson, was just across on the opposite bank.[9] I remember three things above all others at this place: first was the magnificent tulip tree; the second, the joggling-board near-by. The latter was a long, strong plank, with the ends resting on

7. Williams, Govan, 41, M, W, planter, S.C.; Rebecca, 36, S.C.; Mary, S.C.; Dosia, 14, S.C. 9th U.S. Census: 1870. Population Schedules: Louisiana (Rapides Parish).

8. Texada, Thomas J., 35; Martha J., 32; Eliz. L., 15; Martha J., 13; William G., 11; Louisiana, 9; Kate M., 7; Thomas J., 4; Welch, 2. 9th U.S. Census: 1870, Rapides Parish, La.

9. "Bloomfield, near Lamothe's Bridge, was the home of Col. James Dawson before the war. Just after the war there was trouble between Col. Dawson and General Long. General Long went to Alexandria; on his return home when he arrived at Lamothe's Bridge Col. Dawson was coming out of the store at that place. General Long shot and killed him before he reached his saddle horse hitched near the door. A sorrowful story of domestic trouble. General Long was cleared by the unwritten law." Dosia Moore, Melrose Collection, NSU. Lamoth, a post-hamlet of Rapides Parish, is situated on a confluent of the Red River, four miles south of Ashburn, the nearest railroad station, and 9 miles west of Alexandria. Alcée Fortier, *A History of Louisiana*, II, 33 (hereafter cited Fortier, *Louisiana*).

two low posts, and held in place by a strong peg through a hole in each end. Oh, the fun we had "joggling" up-and-down, up-and-down, on this board! Most vivid of all is my memory of their immense, beautiful hall. The ceiling was very high, and there was a graceful arch across the center. The polished floor was wonderful for dancing, and as we grew older, our happy little crowd often gathered there.

My father and mother loved young people, and the boys and girls met at our house, where we romped through all the singing-games and square dances. In summer we loved to gather on the immense front steps and sing the new songs: "Molly Darling," "A Lone Rock by the Sea," "My Poor Heart is Sad with its Dreaming," and "Nora O'Neil." The old favorites were not neglected, as Pere and Mere always called for them.

Sometimes Sister and I went with my father and mother to visit their friends—to Castile, where Captain Louis Texada lived, or to see Captain Joe at China Grove. I loved all the gardens on Bayou Rapides, but for some reason I remember the moss roses at Castile with special tenderness. My father's valiant soldier friend, Dan Haworth, lived at Lamothe's Place, and how I did love to sit by the great fireplace on winter nights and listen to his and Pere's tales of the war![10] Sometimes we went away over to Avoca, on Red River, to see Colonel Stephen Meade and Miss Lily.[11] It was my never-ending delight to watch the steamboats pass in their unbelievable grandeur.

10. Daniel Thweate Haworth and Caroline Ann Robert Haworth had children: Clinton Robert Haworth, Leander Bernard Haworth, Oscar Haworth, Daniel Thweate Haworth. George Mason Graham Stafford, *Three Pioneer Rapides Families* (Baton Rouge, 1946), p. 178.

11. "Mrs. James Jefferies was Miss Lillie Mead, a niece of Mr. Stephen Mead who owned the Avoca Plantation before the war. Soon after the war was over she married Col. James Jefferies. I used to visit her when I was between 5 & 6 years of age. I only know that she was sweet and was loved by all who knew her. She used to reward us for our visit with hot rusks and tea. Avoca is about 15 miles above Alexandria on the left descending bank of Red

Thus quietly passed the days of our new-found peace. Our elders were troubled and harassed, no doubt, but little did they know that Fate held in store for them more suffering and bitterness than they had ever known. An unseen monster was bearing down upon them—Reconstruction.

River. It is just opposite the plantation on which Rapides Station is now on the T & PRR across the river. When Mrs. Jefferies died she left legacies to the Luckett girls. When you come we can go see Mary Texada (she was one of the legatees, and she can tell of the latter part of Miss Lily's life). I only knew her when I was a child. Miss Lillie Mead was near my mother's age. After the war Mr. Stephen Mead died, and Miss Lillie inherited his property. Dosia Moore to Mrs. Cammie Henry, Melrose Collection, NSU.

V

Reconstruction

In spite of all that has been written on the subject, many persons in the North have never understood the condition of the Negro in the South during Reconstruction. They do not know how this race was made a tool in the hands of unscrupulous wretches, to torture, crush, and humiliate the class of whites who had been in the ascendency before the War.

"When water boils, the scum is bound to rise." The terrible civil [war] struggle which had just ended gave the riff-raff of both North and South just the opportunity they wanted to batten on the ruined land-owners of the South. The poor Negroes, ignorant, superstitious, excitable, gullible, were easily bent to the evil purposes of these false leaders. As so often happens during political crises, a low type of white men known as "carpet-baggers" insinuated themselves into positions of responsibility and trust. They eventually led the Negroes into poverty and suffering such as few had ever known in slavery days, and they drove the aristocracy of the South to acts of desperation. The bitterness engendered in their [planters'] hearts at that time will never be eradicated until the last proud old heart is stilled.

The white demagogues were tireless. They were constantly among the Negroes, holding meetings, talking, and working up hatred and prejudice in the minds of a naturally good-natured people. Even those who had had the kindest of masters, and who had proved their devotion through the bitter years of war, were persuaded to leave their old owners, lured away with the empty promise of "forty acres and a mule to every man." Many of the ex-slaves were working for their former owners, either for wages or as "half-croppers," and were contented and happy. If left undisturbed, adjustment would have been simple and natural. As it was, Dr. Sweat's Negroes all left the hills and went to the river. His young son, for the first time, took hold of the plow. Dr. Luckett's hands left Red River and went somewhere else. The one thing the white-trash bosses could not bear was to see the Negroes working peaceably for their old masters. Conditions were very bad on the river, and some of the Negroes were incited to acts of insolence. I firmly believe that of those who lived to the end of this troublous [*sic*] period, not one failed to see that he had been made a catspaw. Many of them openly confessed their mistakes, and bitterly repented.

One of the outstanding incidents of my childhood was the return of old Abra'm, a slave on Dr. Luckett's plantation, who had run away soon after gaining freedom. He had been very offensive, persuading other Negroes to leave their crops, and causing no end of trouble. One day, several years later, a servant came to Mrs. Luckett and told her that Abra'm had come back, was sick, and asked if she would come see him.[1] She was troubled.

"Is he very sick?" she asked the messenger.

"Yes'm, Miss Adeline, Unc' Abra'm sho gine pass out dis time."

Miss Adeline's tender heart melted. "Tell him I'll come," she said.

Then she came to see my mother. She asked if Mere would let Sister and me go with her. It was an unusual request, she

---

1. "Dr. Levin Luckett married Miss Adeline Crain, daughter of Col. R.A. Crain. Oak Hill, where the Boyce hot wells are now, was the home of Col. Crain. A lovely place, [it was] just in the edge of the pine woods and not far from the town of Boyce." Melrose Collection, NSU, III, 22, 23.

knew, but the visit would be something of an ordeal, and she felt that our sweetness and innocence would give her strength, she said. Now Mrs. Luckett was our adored Godmother, and we would have gladly gone through fire with her. We were in a tremble for fear Mere would refuse. To our joy, she consented.

Never shall I forget that trip. There was a clean, "double-pen" log cabin [cabin with open hallway separating the two wings], with a row of china[berry] trees on each side of the walk in front. These were in full bloom, and to this day I never smell the heavy exotic perfume of china blossoms without a little catch in my throat, and I see again the strange drama in a log cabin among the cotton. As we came up to the house the crowd of Negroes in the yard parted respectfully. Mrs. Luckett held each of us by the hand. Old Abra'm was lying on a bed in the corner. Mrs. Luckett spoke to him, and asked how he felt.

"Mighty po'ly, Miss Adeline. I sho God is, and thanky ma'am." He turned his head away, then back again.

"Miss Adeline, is I gine dine?" he asked steadily.

Mrs. Luckett hesitated only a moment. "Yes, Abra'm, I'm afraid so. I won't try to fool you."

"Miss Adeline, will you pray for me?" he asked. At once Mrs. Luckett bowed her head and prayed earnestly for the old man's soul.

His eyes never left her face. When she had finished her prayer, he said, "I been a bad nigger, Miss Adeline, but I'se sorry now. Miss Adeline," he said—and I have never heard such pleading in a human voice—"will you forgive me?"

"Why, of course I forgive you, Abra'm! And the Lord will forgive you, too."

A light came into his eyes. "You and Jesus!" he murmured. "Miss Adeline, kin I jes tech yo' hand?"

Without a moment's hesitation, Mrs. Luckett took his gnarled, black old hand and held it. Then talking softly but clearly, she began to kindle his quick imagination with promises and pictures of heaven.

"Death isn't so bad, Abra'm. Jesus said, 'I go to prepare a place for you. In my Father's house are many mansions. . . .' We will all have mansions there, Abra'm. . . ."

His eyes shining, he drank in her words. So, in perfect peace, Abra'm breathed his last.

Not all of the poor, misguided Negroes came to a peaceful end. Hatred of the whites was carefully planted in their hearts, and kept fanned to a flame by the unscrupulous leaders. They were taught that they had been outraged and abused, and that anything they did to their former owners was justifiable. A more dangerous situation cannot be imagined. To add to their arrogance, they were given the vote, while the white men who had taken part in the war were still denied the franchise. Most of the offices in the state were filled by Negroes or the rascally whites who were inciting them to every sort of crime. In many cases even the school directors were the most ignorant Negroes.[2] At last, the franchise was restored to the white citizens. The citizens could go peaceably about their affairs once more, without fear of being haled into court on some spite charge by the lowest man in the parish.

Although white men had only recently regained the right to vote in elections (I believe it was in 1870 they regained the rights of citizenship) while freedmen were given the franchise immediately on being made free, still Negroes loudly clamored for "social equality" and were egged on by the state government.

2. P. O'Hara, Terrebonne Parish, stated: "In my parish there are twenty-two schools on paper, attended by fourteen hundred scholars on paper, and I tell you there are men there drawing seventy-five dollars a month, who, I pledge my word, can not write their names." *Annual Report of the State Superintendent of Public Education, William G. Brown, to the General Assembly of Louisiana, For the Year 1872.* Session of 1873 (New Orleans, 1873), p. 53.

We had [William Pitt] Kellogg, a carpet-bagger for governor, and [P.B.S.] Pinchback, a Negro, for lieutenant governor.[3] The recently freed slaves were ignorant, malicious, and were ripe for any mischief they could do to "de white folks" of the South. They lost all sense of gratitude to the men who protected and provided for them through the many years of slavery and utter dependence. They ignored the many kind masters, but loved to recall the few who abused the solemn trust of slaveowning. The cruel wrongs of a few overshadowed the Christian kindness, the fatherly care, of the mass of slaveholders.

Our carpetbag government held before the Freedmen the untrue picture of an enslaved race who were abused and hunted like wild beasts. They succeeded in making the Negroes believe that the white people of the South were their natural enemies, and that even now since freedom had come to them the white folks were cheating them out of their rights in many ways.

By getting every voter to the polls, the people in and around the little town of Colfax, on Red River, managed to elect intelligent, educated white men to fill the offices of judge, clerk of court, sheriff, etc.[4] Then a northern man named White came to

3. Statement of S. S. Marshall: ". . . to judge properly of the conduct and motives of the whites in any such case, the peculiar circumstances in which they are situated must not be overlooked. In most of the Red River parishes, the colored population very largely predominates in numbers; their political leaders, to maintain their ascendency, are constantly infusing into their hearts poison and suspicion against their white neighbors. They are taught that the whites are their enemies, and will return them to slavery on the first opportunity. A feverish and unsettled condition of society is thus created." U.S., Congress, House, Reports of Committees, *Condition of Affairs in the South*, 43rd Cong., 2nd sess., 1873, Report 261, Part 1:11.

4. "Grant Parish lies on the north bank of Red River, some three hundred and fifty miles from New Orleans. It was created by the legislature of 1869, having been carved from the territory of Rapides, Winn, and other parishes which surround it; its population is about 5,000; the races are almost equal in number. . . . Colfax, the parish seat, is a small village containing four or five dwellinghouses, two or three stores, and perhaps a resident population of

Colfax. He seemed to be the Fiend in disguise. He immediately began holding meetings among the colored population, inciting the Negroes to every form of insolence and violence. He promised them that if they got into trouble, he would see that the government protected them. Any student of human nature knows the result of such a course.

Whiskey was sold at every crossroads store, and this inflamed crude and untrained minds. While in this state, the Negroes could be led to any length of rashness.

There lived near Colfax a widow and her young daughter. They were gentlewomen, cultured and refined. Their kinsmen had tried to persuade them to leave their place and live with relatives, but they hated to abandon their home. A Negro woman whom they had known always lived in the yard, and they did not feel afraid.

Late one afternoon, they heard ribald shouting up the road. Peering out they saw several Negro men approaching, led by a well-known "bad nigger." It was perfectly clear that they were howling drunk. A few of their words drifted to the unprotected women, and they took alarm. Mother and daughter slipped out the back door, to the house of the old colored woman, and begged her to hide them. She did—and a few minutes later, when the drunken Negroes demanded to know where they were, she handed them over to these monsters. Unnatural woman! Most any other old Negress would have fought to save the white women who had thrown themselves on her mercy.

The mother regained consciousness first. She dragged her daughter into a thicket of briers, and cowered there until the

---

seventy-five or one hundred persons. Before the fight of April 13, 1873, it contained a brick building, which had formerly been a stable, the property of a Mr. Calhoun, to whom the plantation belonged. When Grant Parish was created, and Colfax chosen as the parish site, this stable was converted into a court-house. . . ." *Ibid.*

girl had recovered sufficiently to crawl on hands and knees. They finally managed to make their way into the deep swamp.

Fortunately, their assailants went to a nearby store to get more whiskey. They became too drunk to go back and kill their miserable victims. In their drunkenness, they boasted. Someone with a spark of humanity in his breast heard, and carried the news to the good men of the neighborhood. There were no telephones, but there were fleet horses, and the message traveled from house to house with incredible swiftness. In a few hours, a large party of grim-faced men rode toward the swamp. Still the awful news traveled—up the bayous, up and down the river.

Their first purpose was to save their [the women's] lives. They found them. Almost naked, almost demented, they screamed and ran from their would-be rescuers. Gentle hands caught them, wrapped them in coats. On swift horses they were carried to the nearest plantation home and given every care.[5]

5. Testimony of Robert P. Hunter: "Just after the Colfax affair, and while the Metropolitan Police were in Grant Parish, some eight or ten Negroes—I know this, sir, as a matter of notoriety all over the country—under the leadership of a Negro named Hamp Henderson, went at night to the house of Mrs. LaCour, one of the most respectable ladies in that country, tried to get into the house, and I think succeeded in getting in. Mrs. LaCour and daughter, a young lady about sixteen years of age, I think, who stood as high as any lady in that section of the country, a beautiful young lady, ran out of their own house, and they had (these two ladies Mrs. LaCour and Miss LaCour) a baby; I heard at the time that it was a grandchild of Governor Wells, but I don't know that is so. It is stated, anyhow, that it was a child of Mr. Mumford Wells, Governor Well's son. Mr. Wells was living in that neighborhood; they ran to an old colored woman's house in whom they had great confidence and asked her to protect them; she said, 'No, damn you, you white people have had your day, and now it is our day; protect yourselves;' they run off into the field from there; the Negroes pursued them; they ran into the field, were pursued by the Negroes, who were led to them (it was at night) by the cries of the child. They left the child and ran into the woods. Just as they got into the edge of the woods, they were overtaken by the crowd

Then retribution. The countryside was being combed for the criminals, but as it happened, it was only a small party of white men who finally came upon them. There was not the slightest argument as to what was to be done with them—they were hung to the first tree, the five bodies left swinging.

This was the scalawags' opportunity, and they availed themselves of it thoroughly. To the Carpetbag governor in New Orleans, and to every northern newspaper went the story of this awful "southern atrocity." The poor Negroes were "being butchered." The result of these wild tales was felt immediately. Every white citizen of the parish was removed from office, and replaced by a Negro!

Negroes moved into Colfax daily, a dark sullen stream of them flowing by in the roads, gathering in the town, ominous, sinister. The man, White, armed every Negro. The bearing of the "freedman" grew more and more intolerable and their attitude was soon communicated to those of the surrounding country. Life for the plantation owners became a perilous affair. Work was almost at a standstill, for no man dared leave his family unprotected.

---

of Negroes. Miss LaCour was raped there, in the presence of her mother and those other Negroes, by Hampton Henderson. I don't know, but I heard—it is not a matter of notoriety at all—that Mrs. LaCour, the mother, was raped by all the other Negroes the same time. That was not a matter of notoriety, but the rape of the young lady was. Miss LaCour was a highly respectable young lady; she is, I am now informed, crazy from the effects of it. The condition of affairs in Grant Parish has been disturbed ever since it was created. The Colfax affair was on the 13th of April. I think this must have been about May, sir. It was during the first advance of the Metropolitan Police up there in May 1873. It was while the police were there. The *Ozark*, Governor Kellogg's gunboat, was lying in the neighborhood. . . . There was great excitement about that affair of Miss LaCour at the time, and the feeling among the white people that the Negroes were protected in it by the metropolitan force." U.S. Congress, House, Reports of Committees, *Report on the Condition of the South*, 43rd Cong., 2nd sess., Report 261, p. 511.

Matters grew worse. Negro men in the town, securely intrenched in courthouse or other buildings, shouted the vilest and most insulting threats at white men passing through. This was too much for human endurance. Quietly the desperate citizens began organizing, gathering any and every sort of gun, and collecting every particle of ammunition that could be procured.[6] Their arms were poor at best, for they had only the old shotguns with which they hunted, and their pistols.

April 13, 1873, was the day set for the attack on the Negroes intrenched in the town of Colfax. All the men of our neighborhood had volunteered, but while last plans were being made, it was revealed that no one had been detailed to stay at home and protect the women and children. Of course this could not be, but all wanted to go. At last lots were cast to decide the question. It fell to Captain Louis Texada, Clint Haworth, and my father, to be the home guard. They were bitterly disappointed, but accepted gracefully. The country under their protection extended from the Red Store on Bayou Rapides to Wiel's Store, a distance of about twenty-five miles.[7] The Negro population in

6. S.S. Marshall's statement: ". . . during the week prior to April 13, C. C. Nash, the duly-elected, commissioned, and acting sheriff of Grant Parish, was busy summoning a posse of men to retake the court-house and put down the lawlessness that had filled the parish with terror and alarm." U.S. Congress, House, *Report on the Condition of the South*, 43rd Cong., 2nd sess., 1873, part 2:17. "Mr. Kellogg had learned that bayonets were stronger than popular will . . . commissioned in absolute defiance of popular will R. C. Register, Parish judge, and Daniel Shaw as sheriff. . . ." *Ibid.*, p. 15.

7. "The original Red Store, so named for its color, was a large wooden structure located at the base of Henderson Hill near Brubb's Spring and the dam across [Bayou] Jean de Jean. That it was the original store at Cotile is repeated in tradition. Since the first post office was established at Cotile in 1819, it is believed that the general store housed it." Patsy K. Barber, *Historic Cotile* (n.p., 1967), p. 91. "Weill, a post town in the northern part of Rapides, is situated on Bayou Boeuf, about five miles northwest of Alexandria and three miles south of Rapides, the nearest railroad station." Fortier, II, *Louisiana*, 620. "The white people were so alarmed at the atrocious acts that they called for help from adjoining parishes, which was liberally responded

this area was about double that of the whites, so the task of the home guard was no small one. With conditions as they were, no one knew what to expect.

Never shall I forget that night. The men rode away toward Colfax, and my father and his two comrades took up their vigil. They divided up the territory to be guarded. Pere said he wanted all of his charges in one house; so he could watch them better. We assembled at Mrs. Tom Texada's, as she was not well enough to be moved. There were five or six ladies, with their children, under this one roof. There were two boys of fifteen, and four girls from fifteen to eighteen. Naturally we were in a state of wild excitement and eager to have some part in things. My father, before he left on his rounds, very wisely assigned us something to do.

Regular gun shells could not be bought, and the men used "blue whistlers" in their shotguns. Pere showed us how to make them. We cut pieces of brown wrapping paper and rolled them into small cones. Into this we poured just the right amount of powder; then put in two layers of buckshot, three in each layer. This left enough paper to tuck in snugly and secure the charge. Our young fingers eagerly wrapped these awful messengers of death. Then he showed us how to put the home-made shells into the old muzzle-loading shotguns. Just before one was dropped in, the tip of the cone was torn off to release the powder. After cautioning us not to go to sleep, he left.

There was no danger of our sleeping that night! When Pere had gone, the women sat about and talked in low tones, while we girls made cartridges. There was much discussion as to

---

to. These men, together with citizens of Grant Parish, encamped at a spring three miles from Colfax. C.C. Nash, the elected sheriff of Grant Parish, took command of the white forces, in all about two hundred fifty men. . . ." J.R. McCain, "Looking Backward," typescript in Melrose Collection, bound volume 2, pp. 39-48 (Mr. McCain was a veteran of the Colfax riot).

what would be done should there be an attack. Aunt Mag Texada said that if the Negroes came, her first impulse would be to go out and reason with them. She had never been afraid of them, she said.

About twelve o'clock [midnight], there was the sound of a voice at the gate! We were all talking, so did not hear it very clearly. In the deathly stillness that followed, we heard the gate-latch rattle. There was a rush and rustle in our midst—Aunt Mag and most of the girls had fled out of the back door! They had not stopped to reason: flight was imperative.

Betty Texada and I stood our ground. As the two boys seized their guns, we each swept up a lapful of the "blue whistlers." When they rushed to the dark porch, we went, too. "Get behind the pillars," I whispered. This they did, and Betty and I stood back of them, to hand them ammunition as needed. I did not feel one tremor of fear—it was my young sweetheart who stood between me and danger! What is sweeter than romance in the face of death?

I heard a trigger click. "Wait!" I whispered.

"Who is that?" called one of the boys.

A laughing voice replied, "Govan Williams! Don't shoot me!"

Oh, what a relief! There were exclamations, laughter, and tears.

My father opened his arms wide, and they were filled to over-flowing. My sister was almost fainting with fear, so he sat down and held her close. He was so sorry he had frightened us; he thought surely we would recognize his voice when he first spoke. He praised Betty and me and the two boys for being so quick to protect the house. We felt as if we had been knighted.

Pere returned to his vigil. Exhausted from excitement, we young folk soon fell asleep. When we waked next morning, our band was increased by one! While we slept, a baby was born to Mrs. Texada. There is always this strange linking of life and death—for this was indeed to be a day of death.

Strangest of all, it was Easter Sunday, symbol of resurrection and life! The old gardens were blooming sweetly, the air was filled with perfume and the songs of birds.

The company of stern-faced white men surrounded the town of Colfax. The night before, a Negro messenger had been sent to those intrenched in the town, telling them that if they would give up their arms and go peacefully to their homes, they would even be spared. An insulting answer was returned. In the morning, some of the men wanted to attack at once, but Captain Hadnot insisted on giving them one more chance.[8] He said that if even one would surrender, he should be allowed to go unharmed. He insisted on going himself with an offer of peace. With a white handkerchief on a cane, he walked out into the square. Just as he paused to deliver his message, a volley rang out, and this brave man fell, riddled with shot.

Pandemonium ensued. I will make no attempt to describe this scene of horror. At the close, all of the Negroes entrenched in the town were dead, and many of the white men who dealt out their punishment were wounded. By some strange irony, White, the man largely responsible for the situation, made his escape.

This awful episode, one of the most terrible that ever happened on Louisiana soil, saved us—perhaps the whole state—from utter destruction. Afterwards, an old colored man told that the Negroes everywhere were organized, waiting, watching the outcome of the conflict at Colfax. This was a sort of test case. "It was a good thing the white folks killed those niggers," he said, "or they would have been wiped out." The white citizens knew that it was worse than useless to appeal to the government for protection at that time. There was *no* gov-

8. "The terrible riot of April 13, 1873 (Easter Sunday) . . . originated in the fact that Gov. Kellogg appointed two sets of officials with the view, it is alleged, of bringing about just such a result. . . ." *Northwest Louisiana Memoirs*, p. 498.

ernment in Louisiana, except one of rapacity and ruin; any message to Washington would have been promptly stopped.

The guard camped in Colfax that night. When they were sure that no further trouble would arise, they went quietly back to their plantations and took up life where it had been dropped. For some time the Negroes were subdued and respectful, and went peaceably about their daily affairs.

Those who had stirred up the strife would never permit this to last. Terrible tales of the Battle of Colfax were reported to state headquarters at New Orleans, and every northern newspaper carried great scareheads about the "Louisiana Massacre." The poor downtrodden Negroes must be avenged.

Then a whisper began to creep about—the white "rioters" were going to be arrested and brought to trial. The whisper grew more persistent. The white people knew what sort of trial they would get—a mockery of justice. So, very quietly, the men of our community established a camp in the deep swamp of Bayou Boeuf.[9] A dell, nestling beneath hills in Bayou Boeuf's swamp was their forest home. In the daytime the rousterbouts could ride in and see about their homes, hear the latest news from Alexandria, but when night came they retired to their camp in the woods. So, again, we were temporarily bereft of fathers and brothers. My story of this troublous [sic] time is only that of our own community, the Bayou Rapides neighborhood. My father did not have to hide, as he was one of the home guard and not present at the battle. None of the Negroes

9. "Well, in about ten days notice was received all along the line that U.S. warrants were out for most of us and that the U.S. marshalls were backed up by Metropolitan Police and U.S. soldiers. They came to the town in which the battle had taken place and sent out squads all over the country to arrest the boys. . . . We went to the woods laying out during the day and made raids into town during the night getting ready to get out from there by the light of the moon to the finest country on earth, Texas." "One of the Incidents of My Boyhood," Oscar Watson typescript account of the Colfax riot, Melrose Collection, II, 56-64.

knew the part he played. But all our friends and neighbors except the very old men and young boys had to fly to this refuge. With their usual attitude toward danger they made light of it, and referred laughingly to themselves as "the rouster-bouts."

Soon a U. S. marshall was sent out from New Orleans, and began moving heaven and earth to get a list of the men who had taken part in the battle.[10] In desperation, he approached a lady whose husband was in hiding and told her if she would give him the names of those from our neighborhood, her husband would be allowed to go free. This officer told Mrs. J. W. T., when he made a formal call on her, that he knew her husband was one of the rioters and was in hiding, and that if she would disclose the whereabouts of this forest camp he would assure her that Captain T. should go free; there would be no charge against him. She indignantly refused, telling him if he

10. "The death of Wm. Irvin at Colfax removes the last of the Grant Parish prisoners from this earth. . . . These prisoners were Donas LeMoyne, Clement Penn, Andrew Cruikshanks, Wm. Irvin, and John Pierce Hadnot, and were on trial for their lives under the Ku Klux Act, for participation in the battle of Colfax during the Grant Parish riots. Of these men Irvin and Hadnot were the only ones in the fight. . . . Chief Justice Joseph Bradley decided the Ku Klux act under which they were tried was unconstitutional and set them free. . . ." Milton Dunn to editor of [Alexandria] *Town Talk*, clipping dated 17 March 1914, scrapbook 67, Melrose Collection, NSU. "The steamer *R.L Hodge* brought up to Colfax, last Tuesday, two companies of the 19th Regiment U.S. Infantry, which will be stationed there for some time to preserve order and perhaps to make arrests. These are white troops, nearly all Germans, under command of Major Smith, a Kentuckian. Gentlemen who were passengers on the *Hodge* speak in the highest terms of the officers as gentlemen of honor and intelligence, and say that the soldiers show a liberal spirit towards our people, and express their sympathy with us in our oppressed condition." Clipping from *Natchitoches Times*, 26 April 1873, Scrapbook 67, Melrose Collection, NSU. Testimony of James Forsythe, of Catahoula Parish: "In November 1873 the *Ozark* left New Orleans with some troops for the purpose of trying to capture the Colfax men. I left New Orleans on Sabbath evening. I suppose the *Ozark* left on Sunday." U.S. Congress, House, *Report on the Condition of the South*, 43rd Cong., 2nd sess.,1873, Report 261, Part 3:382.

wanted to capture these men he would find them all together and that they would not be easily taken, and that she would not be bribed.

The country Negroes were afraid to tell. About all that he could get from them was "I dunno." There was a yellow "town nigger" who was bolder. He began secretly making speeches to gatherings of his people, urging them to take a stand for social equality with the whites, and to avenge their wrongs. Kellogg, our carpetbag governor, got [Loyd] Shorter, this Negro, an appointment as U. S. marshall, and he was supplied with blank warrants. If he had a grudge against any white man, he filled in his name, and had him arrested.

When this man rode through the country, it was as if a magic wand had been passed over the colored population. Their courage rose, and even the tone of their songs changed. One of their favorites at this time was "We'll all charge around." Just a line, with this meaningless refrain, made up the song, but the verses were endless in number. "No mo' gittin' up in de mawnin' "—repeated—"and we'll all charge around!" "No mo' whippin' wid de cowhide. . . ."

It could not all be kept in bounds. The women who were house servants would let fall a hint—a word here, a word there, and gradually the white people gathered what was going on under cover.

One story will give some idea of conditions. A young man who had been conspicuous in the battle at Colfax rode a fine yellow horse. Because of the animal's unusual color, his owner lovingly called him "Punkin'." In one of his speeches to the Negroes, Shorter held up a new rifle. "See this gun? Well, I'm savin' a bullet for Bob Whittington! And after I get him, I'm gona carry old Punkin' to Nyawleans for Kellogg to ride!"[11]

11. Testimony of James S. White: Question: "Didn't you go to Governor Kellogg, when in the city of New Orleans, and tell him not to send any troops up to Grant Parish; that, in your opinion, they were not necessary?" Answer:

Toward the latter part of summer a new song began to be heard—at first here and there—soon from every side. The words sounded senseless, but the air was throbbing, persistent, filled with jungle menace. It was sung everywhere, and each singer did his utmost to make it scary. The air was a throbbing, lilting melody that was enthralling, beautiful, and hideous, full of malice and hatred. This awful time is embedded in my soul, and after all these years, this throbbing, jouncing, rippling music is living in my inner consciousness. I can still hear the wild exultant shouts of the malicious singers. It was jungle music pure and simple, no school of music ever taught it.

At first we heard only:

"De Ozark's a-comin', move erlong chillun!" This would be repeated three times, then, "De Ozark's a-comin', move a-a-long!" This was shouted exultantly.

What was "the Ozark"?

Then we began to catch the words of the song—veiled threats of terrible things that were to happen when "the Ozark" came! Finally some of the faithful old negroes told "their white folks," and the secret was out. "The *Ozark*" was a big government

---

"I don't know that I spoke to him of Grant Parish, but I went to see him in relation to the visit here of a man by the name of Lloyd Shorter, who came down on the same boat that I did, and who, I was told by some of the citizens in the parish as I was leaving, was coming here for the purpose of getting troops to go out to the parish, the object and purpose of which would be to annoy our people; and they asked me if I would not go to see Governor Kellogg in relation to this, and I refused; subsequently some gentleman from my parish on the boat insisted that I should go, and volunteered that if I would go he would go along with me. I consented to do so. I went to see Governor Kellogg; told him the representations of this Negro man Shorter, I was satisfied by persons who knew him, were wrong and indiscreet, and to send troops up to the parish of Rapides for the purpose of harassing those people would only create excitement which would do no good to anybody, either white or black." U.S., Congress, House, *Report of the Select Committee on that Portion of the President's Message Relating to the Condition of the South*, 43rd Cong., 2nd sess., 1873, Part 3:577.

steamboat. It was coming soon, and it would bring the "Metropolitan Police."[12] They would arrest all the men who took part in the Colfax battle and carry them to New Orleans. Through Negro officials, the colored population had had the news long before we did. There was much speculation among us, but the older people rather discredited the story.

Then the *Ozark* came. It was at the Alexandria wharf before any of our people knew it. But how the news flew! Messengers sped along the river and up the bayous. The poor "rousterbouts" had begun to relax. Now they had to be hustled away to their former refuge in the swamp. One of the Davide boys had even ventured to come into Pineville the night before and got married. Before daylight, he received the sinister message, "The *Ozark* has come." He left his bride and fled to the inhospitable swamp.[13]

The Negroes were jubilant. They sang more than ever, the words no longer subdued. They flocked into Alexandria and chatted with the soldiers on the *Ozark*. The Metropolitan Police, resplendent in their uniforms and mounted on prancing horses, cantered bravely up and down the river—up one side, down the other, and made forays on either bank of bayou Rapides. They never left what the Negroes called "de big road." Needless to say, they saw never a rousterbout. Somehow, those dark trackless swamps with their tangled vines, swaying

12. "No. 37. An Act authorizing the muster of the Metropolitan Police Force as part of the militia of the State. . . ."Approved March 5, 1873. *Acts Passed by the General Assembly of the State of Louisiana at the First Session of the Third Legislature Begun and Held in New Orleans, January 6, 1873*, pp. 76-77.

13. The following statement does not identify the man in Dosia William's story: "J. Edward David, lifelong resident of Rapides, born March 31, 1850 in Pineville, died July 1923. He played a conspicuous part in the restoration of Louisiana from carpet bag spoilation and Republican mis-rule during the reconstruction era. . . ." Obituary, unidentified newspaper, July 7, 1923, Melrose Collection, scrapbook 67, p. 123.

Spanish moss, and sawlike palmetto did not look inviting to the newcomers.

Meanwhile, the rousterbouts lounged comfortably in their camp, playing cards, telling tall tales, and whiling away the hours as best they could. Some of them were splendid cooks; so they did not suffer. The inactivity soon began to pall. Then, too, fathers wanted to see their families, young men their sweethearts. A few of the boldest began to slip into the neighborhood under the cover of night.[14]

Soon a simple system of signals was arranged. Near the hiding place of the rousterbouts there was a very high hill which commanded a view of many of the homes in the country about. If there were no soldiers in the vicinity, and all was safe, the mistress of the house would hang a white table cloth in an upstairs window. If there was danger, a red tablecloth would be displayed, the men to govern themselves accordingly. Visits-in-the night became the order of the day.

How exciting it was! There is not a doubt that romance flourished, and many love affairs blossomed that would otherwise have never even come to bud.

As our house was one of those nearest the camp, often one of the men slipped in and asked my father if he could spend the night, and have one more sleep in a real bed. Pere and Mere always made them welcome, and my dear mother delighted in cooking good things for them—dainties which men could not prepare in a rough camp.

Once in particular I remember that three of Pere's friends came in to spend the night. He was worried over their coming,

14. "After dark/ Darling/ We have just heard from the Troops. They are between here and Christies. come verry near getting Mr. Pane. I am uneasy about Milton to night. I think he is too careless. You and Mat leave your present hiding place I dont think you are safe there. Fee is staying at the store he will put this in the mail himself. dont come Saturday night you will not be safe. Nothing more me now. Bee." Undated handwritten note, Mr. Milton Dunn, "Reconstruction Days," Melrose Collection, folder 356B, NSU.

as the Metropolitan Police had been unusually active in that vicinity for several days. He urged them to go back to their hiding place. One of the men had a fall from his horse and hurt his leg or hip so that he was quite crippled. He and two others of the outcasts came in and begged to stay one night and have a good rest. My father was rather unwilling for them to take the risk, but Arthur Melder, the one who was crippled, insisted, said his leg hurt so bad when he slept on the ground, and the white flag was flying from Judge Welsh's window; so my father gave a reluctant consent.

After partaking of a good supper the men retired. The members of the family were to stay on guard and look out for the soldiers. The Negro servants had all gone to their homes in "the quarter," so my father and I unsaddled and fed the poor, tired steeds, and my mother and sister prepared supper.

Sister and I were wild with excitement. We thought we could not close an eyelid, but we all must have dozed. Some time in the wee hours we heard a party of men riding in the road. They were near the gate. A squad of soldiers was approaching! Our friends had protested that they could easily make their escape in case of a raid as the place was so thickly screened with trees, shrubs, and vines, but here were the soldiers. The rousterbouts were called, their horses led out ready to run. It was too late for escape. My father hid the three refugees on a little upstairs balcony. There they lay, guns ready, prepared to die rather than be taken. The men at the gate divided. Some went up the road; some entered the long drive through the large, tree-shaded lawn right by the front door. The great house was dark. The deep shade of the large trees covered everything in darkest gloom. The two parties of men—those in the road and those who invaded the lawn—were evidently scared at the still, solemn gloom of the place. The brave Metropolitans did not attack! They turned back, rode off quickly toward Alexandria, and "the episode was closed."

Arthur Melder gave a deep sigh of relief and said, "I'm darned glad they are gone!" My father told them to mount their horses and hurry back to the camp and stay there till times were better. Which they did.

For nearly a year the *Ozark* stayed moored at the wharf, but not a single arrest was made. All this while our poor men had to live in hiding. At last the Metropolitans decided they could gain no glory by capturing "Colfax rioters" so the *Ozark* steamed away. Fathers, brothers, and sweethearts came back home, and peace reigned once more.

When we had Kellogg for the governor of Louisiana, and the famous "Carpetbag" rule was in full blast, there was a Negro man named Loyd Shorter,[15] a lately freed slave. He had been Dr. Cruikshank's dining room servant (he formerly belonged to Mr. Landry Baillio); he was not ignorant as the generality of

15. Testimony of Robert P. Hunter: "There is one case now that I will explain in all frankness to the committee, of a man named Lloyd Shorter, a colored man, who disappeared just about the time; in fact, it was while the Metropolitan Police were there at Alexandria. There is no record of the case at all. It was never known about. I made inquiries, and could not ascertain as parish attorney. I should have prosecuted, and brought before the court for preliminary examination, any man or set of men, if I could have found their names, who had killed him. It is not well ascertained that he was killed. The singular fact of his disappearance is, that both he and his horse disappeared, and no trace of them has ever been found. I don't suppose there is a reasonable doubt but that Lloyd Shorter was killed somewhere, or by somebody, just about that time. That is the only case I know of that had any relation to politics at all. Lloyd was a pretty big politician among the Negroes. He carried his gun around, and if he was killed, I think it was simply because of his own action, and not because of his color or politics. He carried a gun around, and made threats against some men. I heard him make threats myself against them. . . . The metropolitan police were there, riding over the country, and he disappeared just at that time. I don't know anything more about the case. If I could have found his body, or traced a connection with the disappearance to any man in the parish, I should have investigated the case. . . ." U.S., Congress, House, *Report on the Condition of the South*, 43rd Cong., 2nd sess., 1873, p. 517.

Freedmen were; he had been a favorite with his master, and had learned a good deal by association. He was an ardent member of the Methodist Church, not a pure Negro but a "mixed one." He had the class hatred toward the southern white people in a most exaggerated form. He soon became a politician, and was made a United States marshall by the carpetbag administration. This was after the memorable Colfax Riot.

Loyd Shorter was the informer for the government. He made distorted and inflammable representations about the men who were engaged in that awful battle, causing great trouble in the country. The government supplied him with a number of blank warrants. He could insert any name he chose, arrest and carry any man he pleased to New Orleans as an outlaw.

This United States marshal galloped up and down the country roads haranguing the Negroes and seeking to stir up trouble against the white men in all parts of the country. He delayed the arrests he was threatening to make, as he seemed to gloat over his power, and desired to make the most of it. This had been going on for some time, and to try to avoid more bloodshed, a party of the more conservative white men decided to take Loyd Shorter in hand.

They thought to take him to a secluded place, and give him a talk, secure the package of blank warrants which he had, and send him out of the state. So on a day they went to Alexandria to get him. He lived in town at the time. As they arrived in the outskirts of the town, they met him riding out on a fine saddle horse with his son riding behind the saddle. One of the men accosted him and said, "Loyd you must come with us." He said he would, but he would send his little boy home. He helped the little boy to the ground, saying, "Willie you go home to your mother, tell her not to be uneasy about me. I am going with Mr. —, Mr. —, and Dr. —," calling the names of each member of the party.

The men rode into Red River swamp explaining their intention to Loyd Shorter. They told him if he would surrender the papers that he held and would leave the country with an oath never to return, they would care for his family until he could send for them and make a home in a distant state. If he refused to do this, or if he consented, and later returned to this place, death for him would be the result.

He agreed to the proposition, and was greatly relieved, as he thought they intended to kill him when they took him into the deep woods. His conduct had been such that he felt there was no hope for him. He said he would willingly give up his political hopes and anticipations. So he gave up the papers, and while some of the white men were looking them over, one of the younger men who was drinking (in fact he and Loyd were both almost drunk) insisted on Shorter to "take another drink."

The men who were sorting the papers were startled by the report of a pistol shot, and were horrified to see Loyd Shorter fall to the ground dead. These men had never intended to kill Shorter. They would not have dared to do it, as the United States government was fanatically devoted to these new citizens, and the whole force of this powerful government would be turned to their protection. They thought to scare Shorter and make him leave the state, but if they failed to make him leave they would do nothing to him.

We lived in a state of terror, as the Negroes were insolent and insulting in many parts of the country, and their threats against the womanhood of the white people were unspeakable.

In the helpless condition of the ex-Confederates it was almost suicide to kill, or even strike a Negro for any offense. The country was in the hands of the United States soldiers stationed in Alexandria in consequence of the Colfax Riot. So these men were shocked and dismayed at this awful deed. Their own lives were in danger if it became known.

They hurriedly prepared to conceal the body. A physician who was of the party disemboweled the body. They buried the vitals and loaded the body with heavy weights and threw it into the river. I thought it was thrown into a lagoon in the swamp but my sister says it was thrown into the river. They led his horse out on a high bank of the river, shot him, and he sprang into the water and was carried on the swift current far away. They could not leave any of his belongings to be found so they were distributed among the party to be kept out of sight.

This hasty act of a very young man caused much trouble, as every man in the country was suspected of complicity in the deed. But no evidence was obtainable, and after many months the excitement subsided in a measure.

There was no peace as the whole country was under a ban, and the men who engaged in the Colfax battle were hunted like wild beasts. Some few days after his death Shorter's wife received a letter with his name signed to it, containing fifty dollars. The letter was mailed in Arkansas and said he had decided to leave Louisiana for good, was doing well, and would send money for her and her children as they needed it. He gave no address but said he would provide for his family. She continued to receive money for her living expenses till she was married to another man.

The boy Willie is living in Alexandria now. I am sure he can tell of his father's arrest.

I heard this story from one of the men who were implicated in the affair. Each of these men has crossed "the great divide." It can hurt no one now to tell this gru[e]some story; only one was guilty of Loyd's death. That one had a great cause for hatred toward this misguided Negro. His rash act caused great trouble to himself and his friends, and made life harder for us all. People of this generation can form no idea of what life in the South was during the stormy days of Reconstruction. The law that gathered so protectingly about the Freedmen meant nothing to the white people; that is, it was nothing but a menace.

When it became known that Loyd Shorter had disappeared, the excitement in military circles was very great. Negroes were questioned, search was made in every direction, all to no avail. This quest remained one of the questions [that has] never been answered. Never will, but few know the particulars, and we few will never tell the names of those unfortunate men.

In "the seventies," when the men of the South had only lately regained the privilege of the ballot, there was great excitement over the approaching election in Rapides Parish, especially on Bayou Rapides. There were so many Negroes to vote that it was vitally necessary for every white man to be at the election. General G. Mason Graham was visiting in Virginia and expected to return in time to cast his vote for dear Louisiana, but alas! an epidemic of yellow fever was raging in New Orleans and all the southern part of the state. A rigid quarantine was set up by every other state against poor fever stricken Louisiana.

General Graham started home but met many impediments on his journey. He turned back and took another route only to rush into the vigilant quarantine guards and hear the grim order "turn back." They little knew the determination of that stout Scottish heart, a homing pigeon was a joke when compared with General Graham. It was amusing to hear him tell, in after years, of his roundabout journey home. He arrived in time to vote the Democratic ticket, at the polling place near Tyrone, his lovely plantation home on the bank of Bayou Rapides.

VI

Life Goes On: Post Reconstruction

It is beyond human nature to remain forever sad. After the horrors of Reconstruction days had subsided, life gradually began to take on color once more. Sometimes the brightest blossoms are borne on a flower that has been blighted by drouth. When blessed rain does come, the plant swiftly revives, and there is a brief but vivid aftermath. So with us. Wounds healed; our wrecked lives took on new form and flowered richly.

This was especially true of those of us blessed with youth. For years we had lived under an unnatural tension, excitement our daily portion. Suddenly released, there had to be some outlet for youthful spirits. We threw ourselves madly into social gayeties. Though wealth had been swept away, and the splendour of life "before the war" was no more, the older people could not shake off the glamour of the past. Things must still be done in the grand manner.

Nothing could be more typical of the period than the May Ball. This was an annual event, and opened the summer season. Every girl had to have a new dress for this occasion, if never again. The year that Cora Luckett made her debut, the family asked the privilege of combining the two events. So that year the May Ball was given at the Luckett's beautiful plantation home, Ashbourne. This was one of the most renowned places on Red River. It had been given to Cora's grandmother, Adeline Crain, by her father, who was a famous duelist. Guests came from every part of the country, most traveling by boat.

For the sake of variety, these famous hosts [Lucketts] often gave house-parties on board the splendid steamboats that plied the river in those days. I can remember seeing those floating palaces tied up to the wharf beneath an enormous cypress tree—can still hear the gay voices and music drifting out into the night, mingling with the solemn boom of bull frogs.

The great old garden at Ashbourne was filled with rare and beautiful flowers, but somehow I remember clearly only the latticed arbor in the center, over which clambered fragrant honeysuckle and a climbing rose which bore clusters of soft pink blossoms. I even remember the name of the latter—Prairie Queen. I wonder if it is because my young sweetheart told me one day that the roses were just the color of my cheeks?

At this ball, where Cora made her official debut, I think Sister and I must have made ours, unofficially. We were really too young to attend, but, as we were close friends, Mrs. Luckett persuaded Mere to let us go. As became girls so young, our dresses were of white swiss, with Valenciennes lace. With them we wore white silk sashes, tied in the back. No girl presented at court was ever more excited than I that night. Everything was enchanted. I moved in a haze of romance. My schoolmates, Newton, Frank, and Henry had taken on a strange new glamour. I was Newton's partner for the grand march. Could I have known then that he would one day be Governor of our State, I think it would have seemed only the natural sequence, in the grandeur of the moment.[1] And when dear old Judge Sullivan bowed over my hand and asked for a "set;"[2] I felt like the

1. Newton Crain Blanchard, born 1849, son of Carey Hansford Blanchard and Frances Amelia Crain; governor of Louisiana 1904-1908; died June 22, 1922. Paul A. Sompayrac, "Newton Crain Blanchard," *Louisiana Historical Quarterly*, VI, 56-59.

2. "Bertrand, between Boyce and Alexandria, on the left ascending bank of Red River, was the property of Dr. James Bailley Sullivan and his brother

Blessed Damozel.[3]

My little flame dimmed indeed beside Cora's—oh, lovely Cora! How she sparkled that night! With white tulle looped about her like trailing mists, and caught up at one side with a cluster of delicate flowers; with her dark hair piled on her head in a wavy mass, a strand of pearls wound into it, she was a faery queen. Molly Fellows was her close rival. She, too, was dressed in white tulle, covered with silver spangles. Her train was the longest there! Molly's dress gave Monk Wells just the chance he wanted to keep us all convulsed. He was the lightest of foot of all the young men, and right in the middle of the dance, he would skip onto Molly's train and off again, so lightly that she never knew it!

I had only one terrible moment. Newton had asked me for the third set. As it was about to begin, Jim Boles came up and asked me to dance it with him. Newton had not appeared, and I wondered wildly if he had sent Jim to take his place. I hesitated. My face was like fire, my heart made of ice. What was I to do? The music began. "Yes," I stammered. Just as we took our places, Newton dashed up. "Dosia, I thought you promised *me* this set?" he said. It seemed to my horrified eyes that he glared at Jim. They would surely fight a duel! What *would* Pere say if I caused a duel? I could not speak. I must have looked piteously at Newton, for, with a laugh and a sweeping bow, he left the

---

Owen, of Virginia. They bought this place in the early part of the 19th century some time about 1820 or 1824. His nephew John Holmes Sullivan of Virginia became his partner in this property in 1858 or 1860. They owned the place at the outbreak of the Civil War. Dr. James B. Sullivan was a Union man so the place was not damaged by the Federal army. After the overflow of 1866 and several bad crop failures, they sold the place to the Citizens Bank in New Orleans and bought the Lloyd Place on Bayou Boeuff." Dosia Moore's notes, Melrose Collection, III, 22.

3. A reference to the poem, "The Blessed Damozel," by Dante Gabriel Rossetti (1828-1882).

field to his rival. Later in the evening he scolded me, and told me never to go back on a promise. In my relief I did not mind the scolding.

At midnight, Mrs. Luckett served a magnificent supper to the entire company. The long back gallery was curtained and decorated, and there the tables were spread. After supper, Pere came to take Mere, Sister, and me home. I had nothing to say, and Pere asked, "Sleepy, Baby?" I was astonished! Sleepy? I felt as if I would never sleep again!

Most of our entertainments and social activities were not on such a grand scale as the May Ball. We enjoyed them none the less. Particularly vivid in my mind are the "necktie parties." Who first devised the happy plan I do not know, but it was in the nature of a leap-year affair. Each girl selected a bright piece of calico and made a new dress. There was much excited running to-and-fro, and secret comparing of samples, for no two dresses must be alike. Every girl made a boy's necktie out of a scrap of her dress. This was the point of the whole thing. With his invitation, each boy received a necktie—anonymously. After his arrival at the party, he sought the dress to "match" the tie he wore. When he found the wearer of the luck frock, he became her special gallant for the evening. Sometimes the girls prolonged the fun of "matching" by hiding in unexpected places. Dancing always followed. Sometimes the lovely quadrille, polka, and schottische [a round dance in triple measure similar to the polka but slower] gave way to the more boisterous "singing games," an innocent outlet for bubbling spirits. Remembering, I watch our young people slinking about in the dances of today, and my old heart grows cold. Ours is a decaying civilization.

The War had not killed Romance. Our torn hearts still thrilled to gallantry, chivalry, and beauty. The yearly Tournament afforded full opportunity for an outpouring of our love of pageantry. This was a feature of the Parish Fair each fall.

A few years after the War Between the States, the citizens of Rapides Parish got up a Parish Fair, secured a place near Alexandria for the Fair Grounds, had several frame buildings put up and a grand stand overlooking the race track. There were many fine blooded horses in the country. We had a fine race track and race horses from all over the country came to enter the annual races. Above the large room where products were exhibited, there were lovely seats arranged in tiers for the ladies to view the races.

All faded into insignificance beside the tournament. This was held in the morning, and in the evening following, there was a great ball at which the Queen of Beauty was crowned.

The tournament which took place in my fifteenth year is the one that particularly stands out in memory. I must have just discovered love, for everything that happened in that year wears a rosy hue! I don't remember the other events of the fair, but I do know that the tournament was held on the race track. It made an ideal setting. Someone, sometime, had planted Cherokee roses all around the outside fence. During the sad years of the War this hedge had been neglected, and, as is the surprising way of Nature, had become far more beautiful than if it had been carefully tended. It was a trailing mass of green ten feet high, and, this warm October day, was starred with great white blossoms. Against this background, slender-waisted girls in many frilled petticoats were like bright-colored hollihocks. The gay racing gallants in their vivid costumes were spurts of flame.

At intervals, wires were strung across the race track. From each wire, suspended lightly on little hooks, hung four rings. These rings had been wound with red wool, that the spectators might see them more plainly. The contestants carried long, slanted wooden lances. Four "Knights" rode abreast. At the signal, they raced, with lances extended, around the race track, trying to spear as many rings as possible as they rode under the wires.

My excitement began to rise as we drove out to the fair-grounds, on the bank of Bayou Rapides. It was a blue-and-gold October day, and the roadside was lined with goldenrod and asters. I remember that when we drove home that afternoon it distressed me because the flower faces were disfigured with dust, but nothing marred my morning. The grandstand was already filling when we arrived; so we lost no time in finding a seat where we could see it all. When the "Knights" came into view on their prancing horses, I thought my little heart would burst. Four heralds rode out, blew on trumpets, and called the names and titles of each contestant as he appeared. There were many wonderful costumes, but Dave Stafford's was the hit of the day. He was supposed to represent a Comanche chief, and rode his beautiful horse bareback. He was a fine figure of a man, and his close-fitting suit was quite becoming. He received great applause.

Bill Whittington, "the Knight of the Golden Heart," an ex-Confederate soldier now a young lawyer, was victor. In contrast to the many gay colors, his suit was of black velvet, with knee breeches, and a cloak bearing a big heart of gold. When he rode up in front of the judges' stand, trumpets were blowing, and many shouted as the judges proclaimed Bill Whittington winner of the crown. Then there was a breathless pause while he rode across the field to select his queen from among the girls in the grandstand. Which of the girls would it be? I held my breath. Then he stopped and leveled his lance at Lucy Texada, while his voice rang out, "I name you Queen of Beauty!"

Lucy did not have to feign the proper surprise and confusion—for Lucy was in mourning for a brother. It was a real surprise to everyone. She did not even have a flower to throw! One of her friends tore a rose from her bouquet and pressed it into

Lucy's hand. She tossed it to her knight as she rose and bowed. Bill kissed it and wore it over his heart as he left the field. The roar from the grandstand made what had gone before sound insignificant.

Then what scurrying and hurrying! In spite of the mourning, Lucy insisted that she was going to be queen at the ball—and what girl would not have done the same? So her mother hurried into town to have a suitable ball dress made for our queen. She was beautiful and sweet and not a girl envied her the honor that came to her.

My cup was full, for Lucy had asked Sister and me to dance in the royal set—and me not yet fifteen! The hall was a bower of flowers and festoons of gray Spanish moss. At one end was the throne. At the appointed time, Lucy ascended, knelt, and was crowned. Then Bill took her hand and led off in the grand march. This was followed by the lancers, and the eight couples of the Royal Party made up the first set. Then came stately cotillion and quadrille. Never again in life will anything be so beautiful. Oh, youth of today! Do you really know what beauty is?

Our tournaments were kept up for several years. One year Mr. Dave Stafford won the crown and he crowned Miss Goodie Smith of Bayou Boeuff.

The Freedmen were quite tickled at the tournament and got up one of their own, only instead of spearing at rings, they arranged "a gander pulling." They displayed their horsemanship by riding full tilt down the road and grabbing at the head of a gander. Said gander was hanging over the road by his feet with his dodging head and neck well slicked with lard. The knight who could pull the gander's head off got a prize of five dollars.

The whole country shrieked with laughter and our lists were deserted, "sic transit gloria mundi."

VII

Surprises and More Changes

I have seen and heard some strange things as the years have passed by.

The morning after we moved to Elgeeton, back in 1867, Mere was drawn to the back door by some unusual commotion. There she found a gnome-like little creature who looked as if she might be a hundred years old. Instead of a bright head kerchief, her's was a rusty black—but not as black as the beady eyes that peered out from under her brows. She was bent almost double, so that her neck was thrust forward like a turtle's. She was leaning on a stick.

"Whah de new Boss-man?" she whined. She looked suspiciously at Mere.

When my father came to the door she said eagerly, but hesitantly, "Is you gwine let me stay in my cabin?"

"Why, yes," said Pere. "Everything will go along just as before."

"An' kin I pick up chips at de woodpile?" she quavered.

"I'll do better than that," offered Pere. "I'll have a man cut you some wood and put it in your cabin."

She began making a strange whimpering sound, but no tears came. It was more like the complaining of an old dog. "But can't I pick up chips?" she wailed.

"Why of course!" reassured my father hastily. "Pick up chips whenever you want them. And nobody is going to bother you. You go right on doing just the way you always have. Don't worry now."

With that she hobbled off, apparently satisfied at last.

Every day Mere sent food to the cabin of the old crone, whose name, we learned, was Aunt Sally Boston. But my thoughtful mother always instructed the servant who took the provisions not to set food inside the cabin door. In the same way, my father sent wood over to her, and had it placed on the little gallery. She never came to the "white folks' kitchen," never chatted with the other Negroes on the place. If any of them pretended they were going inside her door, she began to scream and rail at them. To the fun-loving creatures, this was a challenge, and they teased her until Pere called them in and gave them a talk. He told them very solemnly that if they did not let the old woman alone, he would have them arrested and put in jail. This added to her mysteriousness. Stories were whispered about.

Aunt Sally was a witch. There was no doubt about it. Some of the Negroes had seen and heard strange things. She even had a black cat. "And it don't ack lak no cat whut belongs to folks!" they said. It was seldom seen except at night, and then its eyes glowed like coals of fire. When someone came up and found the cat on the gallery of the cabin, it would swell out its tail, put up its back to an unbelievable height, and spit in a positively malignant manner. "Dat ain't no cat," said Aunt Rachel. "Dat's jes' de debil in a cat's hide!"

I listened and believed it all implicitly. To my nine-year-old mind, it was a witch's tale come true.

For a year, things went on this way. Then one bitter cold morning Aunt Sally did not appear at the woodpile for chips. Pere sent Lonzy over to her cabin to make her a fire. When he knocked on the door and called Aunt Sally, she told him to go away. When he started in anyhow, she began to scream at him, "Go way! Go 'way, I tell you!" Lonzy was afraid of "the witch," so Pere went out himself and made the fire. She sobbed and protested, but he paid no attention to her. To his surprise, he found she had torn up a part of the floor. Burned it, he supposed.

After he had made her a warm fire, he went back to the Big House and told Mere she had better send her something that would be good for a sick person—something good and hot. Mere had everything possible done for the old woman, but she would permit little. In fact, it was all done under her whimpering protest. She wanted no one in her cabin.

The next morning when the servant called Aunt Sally, there was no answer. When he finally opened the front door, her black cat shot out, spitting furiously. My father was summoned. He found the old woman dead in her bed.

Pere had to force the Negroes to enter the cabin. He had them throw open the window shutters at once, to let in some sunlight. As Lonzy opened the last, he turned and glanced curiously about. Something caught the light over in the far corner. Lonzy took a step nearer, then screeched, "Lawd Jesus, look deah!"

Pere knew that he was really addressing him, so went over to the corner.

There lay a human skeleton. With it were a few brass buttons, such as those worn on Yankee uniforms. My father had the bones buried with Aunt Sally. Poor old creature! What dreadful secret had she carried with her through the years? No wonder she was crazed. During the War there had been a skirmish nearby. Had a wounded Union soldier crawled into her cabin to hide, and, after warning her never to tell, died there? Aunt Sally's secret died with her.

The black cat was never seen again.

Life at beautiful Elgeeton ended in sorrow. My father died suddenly, and Mere broke under the strain. She had not been well for some time, and now Sister and I could see her fading before our terrified eyes. We had always leaned so completely on my strong father that we felt doubly helpless. In writing to the family in South Carolina we told of my mother's condition, and our anxiety. The answer came back that she must come to South Carolina at once, to recuperate. Why she had not died long ago in "those terrible Louisiana swamps" was a mystery, said her father!

Sister and I took this new problem to our old friend, Judge Sullivan at Loyd Hall.[1] He asked only one question: did Mere want to go?

"Oh, yes!" we exclaimed in unison. It was the one thing of which we were sure, for Mere had brightened as soon as she read the letter, and had been almost talkative, since. Then it was the thing to do, by all means, said Judge Sullivan. It could be managed. Sister and I would board with them—"make our home with them," he put it, but when the plan was presented to Mere, she insisted that we would pay board.

We got our mother off on her great trip to South Carolina. It was the first time she had been back since coming to Louisiana in 1860, and she was so excited her cheeks were positively rosy. During the days of preparation she had been constantly talking of her old home, wondering about girlhood friends she hoped to see again.

After she was gone, Sister and I tried to keep very busy. We had everything packed away in the house at Glen Owen where we had moved after my father's death. We took with us only our clothing and a few of our dearest treasures. Then began our life at Loyd. Little did I think, then, that I would spend the

1. Rapides Parish, family No. 1554, Sullivan, J.B., age 61, farmer, born Virginia, two in household, 121 slaves, 30 slave dwellings. Joseph Karl Menn. *The Large Slaveholders of Louisiana—1860* (New Orleans, 1964), p. 333. Sullivan, James, W, M, 81, single, physician, Va.; Sullivan, John H., W, M, 55, single, nephew, lawyer, Va.; Sullivan, Catherine, W, F, 50, S, niece, Va.; Sullivan, Mary, W, F, 48, single, niece, Va., 10th United States Census: 1880, Rapides Parish, La.

greater part of the years remaining to me in this romantic old house! Soon after we moved, I got a little school close by.[2]

Mere stayed two years in South Carolina. Her health was improving steadily; so her people plead that she remain until she was fully restored to her old-time strength. Not many months after she left Louisiana, Sister and I had both married and were living in homes of our own, so there was no urgent reason why she should return. When she did finally come home, Sister and I each had a little son to place in her arms.[3]

The happy years flew by—full, yet uneventful. Then I was left a widow. With my little three-year old boy, my mother and I moved to Alexandria, and took up life again. The next seven years were the hardest I had ever known, but I cannot remember that we were unhappy. By teaching school, I eked out an existence for our little family. My mother sewed beautifully, which was a great help. Our old neighbors were true and loyal, and we passed many happy hours in their company.

Our dear friends at Loyd Hall were growing old. Judge Sullivan was no longer able to manage the big plantation; so he

2. Teachers for Rapides Parish between September 1, 1876 and the close of April 1877 includes "Hineston: Miss Dosia Wilkins, L. DeLacey, A W. Pardee, E.M. Ball, and Thomas Clements." Wilkins is probably a misreading of Williams. *Annual Report of the State Superintendent of Public Education, Robert M. Lusher, to the General Assembly of Louisiana, for the Year 1877. Session of 1878* (New Orleans, 1878).

3. "Married: At the residence of Judge J.H. Sullivan, Lloyd's Bridge, this parish, on August 25, 1878, Miss Mary Williams, daughter of the late Govan Williams, to Mr. Pius A. Baillio." To this union was born Govan Williams Baillio, on June 24, 1879." Catherine Baillio Futch, *The Baillio Family* (1961), p. 146. No. 760-1019: Baillio, Pius A., W, M, 30, laborer, La.; Mary, W, F, 25, wife, keeping house, S.C.; Govan, W., W, M, 1, son, La. *Census: 1880*, Rapides Parish, La., p. 73. "'Clio' was originally the home of Mr. Landry Baillio in the early part of the 19th century. It afterward became the property of Mr. Joseph Hinson. My brother-in-law P.A. Baillio was born at 'Clio.' " Note by Dosia Moore, Melrose Collection, III, 25, NSU. No. 413-445: Lewis, Albert, W, M, 24, married, farmer, Va.; Theodosia, W, F, 22, wife, keeping house, S.C.; John S., W, M, 11/12 July, son, at home, La. Census: 1880, Rapides Parish, La.

employed a young man, a friend of theirs, to take charge of it for him. This young friend owned a smaller place of his own, but money was scarce in those lean years, so a steady salary looked attractive.

Soon afterward, I married this young man, and went once more to make my home with the Sullivans.[4] Of course Mere and my little boy went with me. There was no lack of room in that immense old house.

I lived at Loyd Hall for thirty years—years of peace and happiness. There must surely have been some dark, rough spots in all that stretch of time, but memory is kind—all is gone but brightness and harmony. The Sullivans loved me and leaned on me. As the years passed, the old judge in particular seemed to cling to me.

He had always scoffed at religion, but one day when he saw me reading my Bible, he asked me to read to him. At the end of the chapter, I stopped. "Go on," he said, but presently I saw that he had fallen asleep. To my surprise, however, he asked me to read again the next day.

I told Mere of this, and after that she prayed over the selection of the chapters. Together, in secret, we discussed them. I never made any comment when reading to him, but finally he began asking questions. Inwardly trembling, I answered as best I could. This went on for some time. Then one day, to my astonishment, I came upon the old judge with the Bible in his own hands. A greater surprise was to come.

---

4. "Henry Scott Moore, eighth child of James Brown Moore and his wife, Margaret Jane Rutledge, was born at the old Moore homestead near Forest Hill, Rapides Parish, Louisiana, on September 26, 1847. He must have changed his name to William Scott Moore as he always signed as W.S. Moore. He was familiarly known to his friends and family as Doc Moore. He married the widow of Albert D. Lewis, who before her first marriage was Theodosia Williams, a daughter of Govan Williams. Mr. and Mrs. Moore never had any children." George Mason Graham Stafford, *Three Pioneer Rapides Families: A Genealogy* (Baton Rouge, 1968), p. 29.

About a month later, as I sat alone with my mending, my old friend came out on the gallery. I saw at once that something was the matter. Tears were streaming down his withered cheeks.

"Dosia," he said, "I believe that Christ came to earth and lived, and I believe that he died to save lost men! And I believe that he can save my soul!"

Tears came to my own eyes. I could not speak. He sat down by me and took my hand in both of his. He talked on and on. He said he wanted to become a member of the church, and in the little time remaining to him, try to make up for some of the wasted years of his life.

When the question of church was broached, there was trouble. Miss Catherine and Miss Mary were staunch Episcopalians, and held that their brother could not possibly join any other church. This was impossible, Judge Sullivan said, for he was going to be really baptized. He had looked up the word in the original Greek, and there was not a shadow of a doubt that Christ was immersed. After waiting all these years, he was certainly going to follow Christ as nearly as he could, and not be led astray by some ignorant interpreter of the Bible.

The sisters called in their minister, and, after much discussion, he agreed to immerse Judge Sullivan if he would join the Episcopal church. When I heard this decision, I was filled with dismay. I looked at the short, plump minister, and at Judge Sullivan's gaunt height, and felt forebodings. They were justified.

There was a great crowd gathered to see the "old Judge" baptized. He was dressed meticulously, and as he waded out into the bayou he was the soul of proud dignity. The nervous minister held up his hand and pronounced the words of the service. He managed to plunge the tall old judge under the water—but, inexperienced in such matters, he could not raise him up again! There was a breathless stillness. Then the old man struggled free of the minister's grasp, and, sputtering and gasping, rushed up the bank.

There was an audible titter from the crowd. Tears of rage filled my eyes. I, too, hurried away, and caught Judge Sullivan just as he was getting in his carriage. Without a word I wrapped his cloak about his gaunt, wet figure, and sat with my arm about him as we rode home. I had been filled with a sort of holy joy over the conversion of my old friend, and now a bungling minister had made a burlesque of his baptism! In the bitterness of his humiliation, he might turn away from his new-found religion.

My fears were unfounded. The matter of baptism was never mentioned. He continued to read his Bible and to bring certain passages to me, over which we had lively discussions. So after all, the old judge had found peace.

Judge Sullivan's health failed rapidly. The plantation became more and more of a burden to him. At last he proposed that my husband buy it, so that he would not have to give a single thought to business affairs. He would make the terms such that they would not be difficult to meet. So Loyd Hall passed into our name, as it had long been in our hands.[5]

Miss Mary and Miss Catherine always seemed grateful for my little attentions. Each of them had often told me, "When I

5. Sale and Mortgage from Mary E. Sullivan to William S. Moore: land with buildings and improvements thereon on right descending bank of Bayou Boeuf, purchased by this vendor through her agent John H. Sullivan from John O. Pickens, agent; also land she purchased from . . . . $9680. "It is understood to be a condition of this act of sale that the said vendee obligates himself to give the said vendor a home in this house & board during her life or as long as he owns the property now conveyed." Rapides Parish, La. Conveyance Book Q, p. 570. Will signed 31 July 1886 at Loyd; probate date April 12, 1902: his estate consisting entirely of one item, to wit: A claim against the U.S. government for property taken and destroyed by U.S. troops during late civil war. . . . $100.00. 9 October 1901. Rapides Parish, La., will of James B. Sullivan, New docket No. 961. John B. Sullivan sworn, January 1,

die, everything I have is yours Dosia."[6] I gave little thought to these promises, but after they died, when their wills were read, I found that they had indeed left me all of their handsome old silver, furniture, and books. This was a great blessing to me, for while Mere was in South Carolina, the house at Glen Owen had burned, and with it, all our earthly possessions.

Thus I slipped into the life of the great old house, so that when I became mistress in truth, there was no change, no readjustment necessary. I only missed my dear old friends whom I had loved so long.

1875. Cotton planter of Rapides Parish; was an army surgeon under General Jackson, 1829, served until 1836, resigned to take charge of a plantation he bought in 1832 in Rapides. Was a Unionist and imprisoned during the war. U.S., Congress, House, Reports of Committees, *Condition of the South*, 43rd Cong., 2nd sess., 1873, Report 101, p. 88.

6. Rapides Parish, La., Olographic will of Miss Mary E. Sullivan, dec's March 1895, large number of bequests including her silver to Dosia Moore, also her books.

VIII

Life At Loyd Hall

My years as mistress of Loyd Hall were full and happy. There must have been cares and irritations, but in retrospect my life is wrapped in a golden haze of peace. Certainly there were not the little bickerings that we hear so often today. Now when young married people begin complaining of their in-laws, I tell them my story of the visit of the three mothers-in-law.

Mere lived with me. My husband's mother had just come to spend the summer, when one day we received a letter from the mother of my first husband, asking if she might come. Why, of course, we agreed at once. When my neighbors heard of it, there was much laughter and speculation as to how the three would get along. They need not have worried. Each old lady had her own room, and did not have to be with the others unless by her own desire. As a result, they were eager for each other's company and spent their days together, quilting, knitting, and tatting. Always they were talking, talking. They had much in common, it seemed, and were in perfect accord. When busy about the house I could hear them laughing and chatting. So the famous "visit of the three mothers-in-law" was a success.

Perhaps people cannot live together in harmony these days because most houses are too small. From constant friction, nerves become sore and sensitive. There is no possibility of complete withdrawal, which is so necessary for composure of soul.

Loyd Hall was an old two-and-a-half story red brick house, built on the generous lines of those fabulous "before the war" days. There were many rooms. Wide galleries upstairs and down were supported by rows of white columns, these in turn connected by graceful cast iron balusters. The rooms were enormous. Even with the massive old furniture, they did not look at all crowded. The tall chimneys at each end seemed to add to the great height of the house.

A grove of giant oaks and pecans swept down to Bayou Boeuf, leaving only space for the sandy road between. At the entrance there were two immense gate posts, with big gates between, and at each side a little gate for persons on foot. How happily this portal swung open to our friends! Even strangers were not turned away. Though he never voiced such religious sentiments, my husband evidently feared we might close our gates to "angels unawares."

Never shall I forget the winter night we gave up our own beds. Two teachers from a nearby school had taken a crowd of boys and girls to a sugar-house party. Returning that night, they had trouble of some sort—perhaps the team gave out. At any rate, we were awakened from sleep about two o'clock in the morning with the request that we take them in. It was a bitter cold night, and they were nearly frozen. We already had the house almost full, but a "doubling-up" began. Finally all were provided for except three girls. My husband whispered to me. I soon had the three shivering girls tucked snugly in our own warm bed. This incredible man had asked that we sit up the remainder of the night to give comfort to these strangers! This we did. He piled fresh wood on the fire and we made coffee. There we sat and talked, and played backgammon, and dozed, until daylight.

At Loyd the day began when old Uncle Ant'ny came shuffling in and made the fires. Then little Tillie brought morning coffee. Oh, nectar of the gods, you could not have surpassed that bracing sip of coffee! I would have one more tiny nap, and then I was ready to face anything. By the time I reached the kitchen, the tantalizing smell of bacon was inviting sleepers to awake, arise. In those days breakfast was a real meal: steaming hot hominy—"grits" they call it now—with bacon, ham, or fried chicken. Then either hot biscuits, waffles, or battercakes, with butter and sugarcane syrup. Coffee, of course. The menu varied little. Men could not have subsisted, then, on a flaky breakfast food, toast, and a poached egg. Even when they did not work, they played hard.

As on all plantations, there were plenty of Negro house servants. Measured by standards of modern efficiency they might have fallen short, for they were often slow, but they finally got the work done, and, usually, done well. It was accomplished without hurry or strain. Occasionally, difficulties arose. I remember once when the fate of a Christmas dinner hung in the balance.

Morning coffee had been served as usual, when the Negroes from all over the place began arriving to say, "Chris'mas Gif'!" and to receive some remembrance, if only a handful of fruit and candy. According to his custom, my husband placed a keg of whiskey where it would be accessible to all, hung a dipper by it, and told them to help themselves.

At breakfast, Ella, the cook, was a little too voluble, and dropped a cup or two, but she managed to get through the meal. She had never fallen by the wayside, so I felt no uneasiness. The big brick kitchen was separate from the main house, connected with it by only a covered walk. Usually Ella had someone else carry the dishes to the dining room, and they had to move almost in a trot so that the food would not get cold on the way. This morning breakfast was rather lukewarm, as Ella had to do it all. When I inquired as to her lack of help, she stuck out her lip. "Dem triflin' niggers sho is takin' Chris'mas!" she said. Still I did not become alarmed.

About an hour later when I went into the kitchen to give some instructions as to dinner, there was an ominous stillness. The range was cold. I began looking in cupboard and pantry—the enormous dressed turkey sat in state, just as it had been left the night before! Dinner was to be at two o'clock, and we were expecting fourteen guests. There began a wild search for Ella. Finally I found her, fast asleep *under my bed*. We managed to get her off to her cabin, and Ben Coleman was called in. He was a faithful Negro servant who had been on the place for many years, and was a very good cook.

He was quite reassuring. "Yas'm, I'll cook dat dinner. Don't you worry. Ella ain't never seed de day she could best me on cookin' turkey an' giblet gravy." I thought his tongue sounded too big for his mouth, but said nothing. He sat down by the kitchen table. "Now les see—for de dressin' I wants onions an' red peppers an' sage—" his voice began to drag. "Onions an' red peppers—" then his voice stopped altogether. I had been looking over the food to see if everything was assembled. I glanced around. Ben's head was resting on the table, his arms dangling.

Big Lloyd White—as black as a coal—came to the door just then, and was very indignant. "You des wait till I gits dis drunk fool nigger outen here, Miss Dosia, an' I'll cook dinner for you."

I felt some misgivings, and when Lloyd returned and began making the fire in the stove, I saw they were justified. I said, "You just make me a good hot fire, Lloyd, an then you can go on. I can cook dinner."

This he would not hear. "I ain't goin' to have Old Miss cookin' no dinner. You des go on in de big house, Miss Dosia, an' leave it to ole Lloyd." When he started across the kitchen he almost fell over his feet.

At last my patience was wearing thin. So I went in the house and told my husband that if he would clear the kitchen of drunk Negroes I would cook dinner. Very quietly he dismissed them all, then disappeared. In a short while he came back with

Buck, a perfectly sober Negro. He had borrowed him from a neighboring plantation "where they haven't got so damned much Christmas," he said. Buck was not a skilled cook, but under my direction he got along very well.

Dinner was ready on time, and, amid much laughter, I told the story of my morning's adventures. I have long ago discovered that the surest way to dispel irritation is to relate the cause to someone else. Almost invariably the tragic mask is turned, and comedy shows his grinning face. My faithful little Tillie helped Buck serve, and the guests seemed to enjoy the food that had been prepared under such difficulties. My husband solemnly swore that never again would the Negroes be given their Christmas keg of whiskey. But another Christmas was a whole year off.

We not only had the Negroes to deal with, but Indians, too. There was a fair-sized Choctaw village in the sand hills not many miles away.[1] In the fall, numbers of them came down to the river to pick cotton. They brought their women and children, and were allowed to camp on the place. They were steady workers, and were welcomed by the planters. They had come to know and trust my husband and me.

One drizzly, sleety day in late November they sent to the house for someone to come weigh up their cotton. My husband

1. Letter from J.W. Dorr, 1860: "The Choctaws have two small villages in this parish, on Bayou Boeuf and Bear Creek of about eight and thirty inhabitants respectively." J. Fair Hardin, *Northwestern Louisiana: A History of the Watershed of the Red River, 1714-1937* (Louisville and Shreveport, n.d.), p. 441 (hereafter cited Hardin, *Northwestern Louisiana*). Somewhat earlier, J. Brooks, Indian Agent on Red River, Natchitoches, wrote to John H. Eaton, Secretary of War: "I beg leave also to state that there are now on Red River and its tributary waters, upwards of three hundred Choctaw Indians, according to their own account, and of whites best acquainted with their numbers. They hang upon the borders of the white settlements, in the most abject state of poverty and wretchedness. . . ." "Letters Received by the Office of Indian Affairs, 1824-81. Caddo agency, 1824-1842" (National Archives, Washington, D.C.), Microcopy 234, roll 31.

was away, so a friend, who happened to be present, volunteered to go out and attend to the weighing. He said, "All right, bring up your sacks."

Not an Indian moved. Finally, Pierre, who was somewhat of a leader, said, "No. Dosia weigh cotton."

Mr. Alexander explained that the weather was too bad for me to come out, and that he would weigh up for them. They shook their heads. "Dosia weigh cotton," said Pierre.

Patiently at first, then in exasperation, the friend went over his explanation of why he was there. The Indians did not argue, not a face changed expression. Only Pierre spoke, the same answer. Mr. Alexander came back to the house fairly sputtering. "Do you know," he said, "those fool Indians won't let me touch their cotton?"

Dosia weighed cotton.

My duties were many, superintending house and gardens, but still there was time left on my hands. One day when several neighbors were present, I suggested that we get up a loan library so that we could keep up with new books as they came out.

"We could pay dues," said someone.

I had a better idea than that. "Let's give entertainments and charge admission. We could raise enough money to buy any number of books."

This plan met with enthusiasm, and a few nights later a crowd assembled at my house to work out the details. We would have to have a stage. Very well, one could be built at the back end of our immense hall. My husband had the stage put in right away, and while it was under construction we ordered some plays.

Everything worked out beautifully. Friends came from the neighboring plantations and from the little town of Cheneyville, five miles away. There was quite a bit of real talent among the players, and the programs were excellent—at least they were highly satisfactory to the audiences which assembled. There were songs and tableaus, and what a ransacking of ancient trunks and chests for the costumes! Lovely old silks, laces, and velvets were worn with conscious grace. Sometimes the plays were uproariously funny, and the rafters rang with laughter.

After the program we always served refreshments, these, too, being sold to raise money for the library. Then there were rehearsals. What fun we had getting up those plays and giving them! I remember the night that tall handsome Robbie Johnson sang "Old Black Joe." We blacked his face and made him a wig of Spanish moss. I snatched up a coat, turned it wrong side out to make it look dilapidated, and put it on him. When he crept out on the stage and sang he was the hit of the evening.

When the entertainment was over and the guests departing, there was trouble. One of the girls said that Pa's coat was missing! I slipped around, turned the coat Robbie had worn, then rushed in announcing that I had found the lost garment! It was a narrow escape. The library flourished, and everyone was plentifully supplied with reading matter.

There were parties. Even before my son grew up, young people loved to come to Loyd Hall, and most of the time the great old house was filled with their chatter and happy laughter. They rode horseback, hunted, fished, swam, and danced. Then there were serenades. Several of the boys and girls played stringed instruments, and a number of them had good voices. A strong team would be hitched to a big wagon filled with hay, then the laughing crowd would load in. I was the favored chaperone, and usually went with them. They stopped at the houses of friends and sang, with banjo and guitar for accompaniment, and the cocks were crowing before they got around the neighborhood. How sweetly their clear young voices rose in the still night air! The old songs were the favorites: "Nellie Gray,"

"Lorena," "Annie Laurie," "Silver Threads Among the Gold," "Maggie," "I was Seeing Nellie Home," "Darling Chloe," and many other tuneful old melodies. In later years, when "In the Good Old Summertime" and "In the Shadow of the Pines" came out, they immediately became popular. Sometimes comedy was introduced by the singing of "Chicken," "Hot Time in the Old Town," "Noah Built the Ark," "Turkey in the Straw," "Po' Moaner," and others of a lively nature, but these were generally sung by the boys only.

Another favorite lark was a sugarhouse party. At that time the cane industry was flourishing, and there were many sugar refineries [sugar houses] scattered about the country.[2] Again the hay wagon was requisitioned, and the party rode joyously to the sugarhouse. The nights were usually cold in late November and December, and the glow of the furnaces was welcome. There was a platform raised above the vats, with a railing around it. Here visitors could stand and watch the busy scene below.

The most fun came when the contents of a vat had finished cooking and a "run" was made. Quite a bit of the contents clung to the sides, and was almost the consistency of candy. This was called "queet," and visitors were allowed to eat as much of the delicacy as they chose. Everyone brought fruit and nut-meats strung on stout thread, and these were dipped into the hot candy, which gave them a delicious coating. Nothing made at home or bought from a store could taste so good.

The peak of the year was reached when we went out to the hills in summer and camped.[3] In the first years it was Belle

2. "Sugar cane achieved a major importance as a crop shortly after cotton, and by 1860 there were 32 sugar houses in Rapides, extending as far up the river as Colfax." Louis J. Daigre Associates, *The Overall Economic Development Program for Rapides and Grant Parishes, Louisiana* (Alexandria, La., 1966), p. 13.

3. "These piney and elevated regions are, with reason, accounted very healthful, and many of the planters of the valleys have their summer

Cheney; later, Hobson; but the setting was much the same in both cases. There was a big comfortable house of rough pine plank. It had an open hall through the middle both ways, which gave the summer breezes full play on hot days. There were other similar cottages nearby, and congenial neighbors came out at the same time, so there were always plenty of young people on hand to take part in the frolicking. The houses were placed in a beautiful natural grove, but in the open spots log platforms were built up several feet high and covered with earth. On these, big bonfires of pine-knots were kindled each night, throwing a lovely light over the entire grounds.

There was a continual round of gayety. The creeks were filled with fish, and there were always some guests who enjoyed the sport of catching them, but if everyone felt too lazy to exert themselves, the Negroes caught plenty for us to eat. There was swimming. The girls went in first, then the boys—oh, never *together*! During the heat of the day everyone played cards or slept.

Evening was really the best of all. There was a big pavilion, and always someone to play a violin, guitar, mandolin, or banjo—or all four of these instruments—so there was dancing. When tired of this, the crowd gathered, forming a huge ring in the flickering firelight, and everyone had to tell a story, recite, sing, or offer some form of entertainment. Sometimes, several combined forces and got up impromptu playlets and charades that were highly amusing.

---

residences there—rustic, but in many instances, spacious and even elegant resorts, to which they retire when the heated term renders their lowland estates uncomfortable if not unwholesome residences, and where they pass the summer in the undisturbed ease of thoroughly rural *dolce far niente*, varying the monotony by occasional visits to their plantations, and with the small excitements, picnics, and taking fish from the abundantly stocked streams, bayous and ponds." Hardin, *Northwestern Louisiana*, p. 439.

And the square dances! Usually the people who lived around the neighborhood were invited to come and take part in these, for often they knew sets and figures which were new to our young people. How joyously they entered into them, and how charming the scene there beneath the arching boughs of beech and magnolia. There was the peavine, the reel, cotillion, and quadrille. For variety they played the old-time singing games. I can still hear their happy voices ringing out:

Can't get a redbird, skip-to-my-loo,
Can't get a redbird, skip-to-my-loo,
Can't get a redbird, a bluebird'll do,
Skip-to-my-loo, my darlin'.

IX

A Feud and An Indian

One day in early fall when we were living at Loyd Hall, a party of men rode up and said they wanted to see my husband about picking cotton for him. The group consisted of two men and two boys about fifteen and eighteen years of age. We had several hundred acres in cotton, and it was rather difficult at times to find a sufficient number of pickers, so my husband was glad to get reinforcements.

The father of the boys, who gave his name as Hamilton, said they would take a cabin for the season, keep house, and pick cotton to make expenses. They had a pair of fine young mules, and a new wagon, in which they carried a camping outfit. They got the house.

These men seemed to be gentlemen, and talked entertainingly, so my husband soon began dropping in and chatting with them at their camp almost every evening. One evening Mr. Hamilton looked troubled. He said he appreciated William's kindness to them. "I can no longer deceive you," he said. "I will trust you with my sad story, and if, after hearing it, you want us to leave, we will go." This was his story:

There had long been a deadly feud [in Claiborne Parish] between the Ramseys and the Tuggles, who were related.[1] Fourteen or more men had been killed, and a bitter hatred

1. John R. Ramsey, deputy clerk and recorder of district court of Claiborne Parish, married in 1854 Miss Sarah E. Tuggle, daughter of Thomas H. Tuggle. *Northwest Louisiana Memoirs*, p. 447.

existed between the two families. On a day when Joe Tuggle and his brother Hamp had gone into town, one of the Ramseys, a cousin of the Tuggle brothers, shot Joe Tuggle. He fell into his brother's arms. Hamp Tuggle, clasping his dying brother in one arm, shot his slayer dead. After this, Hamp, the only survivor of the tragedy, was sought by the officers of the law. He was arrested, but was let out on bond, and went home to his wife and three children.

One day a friend sent him a warning to "keep close," as some men were planning to waylay and kill him. He and his two sons went on with their crop, and minded their business, but one night when his younger son rode down to a stream to water his horse, he was shot from ambush, receiving a wound in the arm. Mr. Tuggle took his two sons and, accompanied by his brother-in-law, slipped out of the country that night. His lawyer advised him to keep out of the way until the other side quieted down; then he would arrange for him to have a trial. The Ramseys, who were wealthy, were determined to go to law with it, and have Mr. Tuggle either hanged or put in the penitentiary. He did not want to resist officers, but was anxious to evade arrest until his lawyer advised him it would be safe to go back to Homer and give himself up.

He was a poor man, so it was necessary for them to work to pay expenses; therefore, the cotton picking. My husband sympathized with him, told him to keep the cabin as long as he wanted it; that he would give him work and help him all that he could.

Mr. Tuggle played the violin well, and often the four of them would dress up and come spend the evening at Loyd. They also visited at my sister's home nearby. We all enjoyed hearing him play the violin.

After cotton picking was over, Mr. Tuggle began hauling cotton-seed to the railroad station. One day, while waiting near the track to unload his cotton seed, a passenger train stopped.

114

Judge Blackman was on it, sitting by a window.[2] He looked out, and, recognizing an old schoolmate, shouted, "Hello, Hamp! What are you doing here?" Mr. Tuggle swung on the train, quietly explained the situation to Judge Blackman, and asked him not to tell anyone of having seen him. My brother-in-law, Mr. Baillio, told Mr. Tuggle that it was dangerous for him to be about the station as so many travelers passed through he might be recognized at any time. He thought that he would be safe if he stayed in the wagon, and his boys could attend to the shipping of the seed.

Meanwhile, trouble was brewing. A letter written by a young man from north Louisiana who was working for my brother-in-law told a friend in Homer of the mysterious stranger who was working at Loyd. He described the man. His friend made some inquiry about it to the sheriff. The sheriff at once sent the description and a warrant to a deputy at Alexandria. Mr. Tuggle knew nothing of all this, so pursued the even tenor of his way, but he and his sons always went armed with a pistol and a shotgun.

One day his wagon had just crossed Loyd's bridge on the way to the station when a horseman rode down to the bridge, fell in behind them, and slowly followed the wagon. Mr. Tuggle felt uneasy. He said, "Elmo, look behind us. That man is after me." The man did not try to overtake the wagon, only loitered along behind them. When they were nearly to Lecompte, Elmo said, "Papa, you are watchin' the man behind us, but you better look in front." A livery stable hack with two white men and a Negro driver had eased in ahead of them. It drove slowly along in front of the wagon.

Mr. Tuggle slipped from his seat, and walked along by the heavily loaded wagon, watching for a place where he could slip

2. Wilbur Fisk Blackman, judge of the Twelfth Judicial District, was born in Georgia in 1841. He lived at Homer, La., and died in 1873 in Shreveport, La. *Northwest Louisiana Memoirs* p. 550.

through the wire fence by the side of the road. He did not hurry, but walked quietly along with his shotgun in his hand. Just ahead, he saw a turn in the road that would hide him for a minute. "Bud," he said, "I'll leave you here, and try to get away, but if these men get me, I want you to promise me to let this thing drop. I don't want you to get in any trouble. Just let them alone."

The boy replied with tears streaming down his face, "Like hell I will! If they kill you, I'll kill one of them before they get me!" Elmo was fifteen years old. No wonder those old feuds died hard!

Mr. Tuggle walked through the field, keeping the hack in range of his shotgun. The deputies had Winchester rifles. He thought if he got far enough from them his shotgun would not reach them, but their rifles would carry so far he would be at their mercy. The men in the hack saw his advantage and did not begin shooting, although they saw Tuggle leave the wagon. Afterward, the hack driver told that the deputies said their "life insurance was not attended to" so they would return to Alexandria and make these arrangements, "and we will come again and get him." "Naw suh!" the driver reported himself as saying, "*we* goin' to come no mo'. You gentmens can come but *not Dutch*, naw Sir! Um got enough right now."

The livery hack drove briskly off towards Alexandria. Mr. Tuggle glided into the swamp back of the field, and disappeared.

That evening I was in the dining room at Loyd. Supper was over; the servants were gone, and I was alone. Suddenly my husband and Mr. Tuggle stepped into the room through one of the French windows. Each carried a shotgun on his shoulder. William told me of Mr. Tuggle's trouble, and that he was going to hide him in the attic. He said that if the officers came in search of him, he could retire to the hiding place.

In the third story of the house at Loyd there was an opening in the south wall, just at the head of the second flight of stairs. This opening led into the loft over the upstairs gallery, with no footing but the joists to which the ceiling of the gallery was attached, just a dark hole which we never used or even explored. If danger came, Mr. Tuggle could go into this dark hole, a piece of furniture be placed over it, and no one would suspect that it was there.

I hurriedly prepared a bed in the garret. Mr. Tuggle took possession, and I sent up his supper. During the time that he was in hiding, my husband and I carried him his meals with our own hands, for we dared not let the servants know that he was hidden in the house. One of the maids complained that there "sure was a heap of dishes to wash every morning. We told an interesting story of our indulging in midnight suppers, and as we often did sit up till the "wee small hours" the excuse was good.

The deputy sheriffs searched about the neighborhood, but never thought to suspect Loyd Hall. After a time, the excitement quieted down. Mr. Tuggle's lawyer wrote him "not to be taken, but to get home and give himself up." He could not pass through Alexandria, as they were on the lookout, and he did not know the country well enough to find his way through the woodland trails.

My husband had a faithful Indian friend, a Biloxi named Banks, who knew every swamp and stream in the country. He could guide Mr. Tuggle to a little-used ferry of which William knew, where his wagon could be carried across on a flatboat. He would then be in Grant Parish, and from there could find his way home. By another Indian, my husband sent word to Banks to come at once, that he needed him. That night when Banks came, I went out to the gate with my husband. The Indian's salutation was, "Friend, who do you want me to kill?" It was said as calmly as if he had greeted him in the usual way.

William explained what he wanted Banks to do, and as Mr.

Tuggle and Elmo were ready, they got in the wagon and started at once. The younger boy and Mr. Tuggle's brother-in-law had left some time before. Elmo had stayed quietly at my sister's home. Banks, on his horse, silently led the way, and the wagon drove off. The Indian guided him across the river, and from there Mr. Tuggle reached Homer in safety, gave himself up, stood his trial, and was cleared.

Thus ended the Ramsey-Tuggle feud.

When I tell my grandchildren this story, they always say, "But Grandma, weren't you scared?" Then I tell them the story of my great-grandmother's shift.

Her name was Susie Keadel and she was a young girl living in South Carolina during the Revolutionary War. Her mother raised flax, and the Negro slaves prepared and spun it, and wove it into snowy linen. In spite of war times, Susie and her mother were making fine garments of the new linen, and storing them in the great cedar hope-chest for her.

One night, when Susie was fourteen years old, the English made a raid on the place. They took some webs of the previous linens which were bleaching on the hedge. They took all the home-cured meat in the smoke-house. Then they went in the house to find something in which to carry away their meat. One of the men spied the open cedar chest. Right on top was a strong new linen chemise that Susie had just finished. With a laugh, one of the soldiers snatched it up, tied a thong around the end, and dumped the hams and bacon into the improvised sack. With much jesting, they took their departure.

Susie was enraged. Despite the pleas of her mother, the next morning she mounted her fast saddle-horse and rode to the camp of the British soldiers. Arrived at Orangeburg, she asked for the commanding officer. With snapping eyes she told her story. The officers gathered around admiringly. When she had finished, the commander ordered her things returned. Sheepishly the soldiers brought up the meat and the raw linen.

But Susie was not satisfied. That new chemise, with its many fine stitches, was missing! "They took one of my garments, too," persisted Susie. There was much whispering and nudging, and a few guffaws. The commander took it all in, then he rose. "Damme, boys, give the gal her shift!" he said sternly. It was produced at once, and Susie rode home in triumph, followed by the bearers of the stolen meat and linen.

When I reach the point in the Tuggle story where the men come into the house with their guns, my youngest granddaughter always wails, "But Grandma! Didn't you try to keep out of it?"

The very idea! I never wanted to keep out of anything in my life.

In the long past days before the Civil War had swept our Southland with torch and sword, Mr. Moore [Dosia Moore's father-in-law] had a beautiful little home on Hurricane Creek near where the town of Forest Hill now stands. There was a large school at this place known as the Rapides Academy. Many of the teachers boarded with Mrs. Moore. There were no railroads or towns near, and the Old Texas Road was the only artery of travel or commerce.

At the outbreak of the War the school was done away with, the place was quiet and secluded. Mrs. Moore's home was the scene of many gay house parties as their friends and relatives in and near Cheneyville were many. Mrs. Moore's family consisted of one grown son, many daughters, and two little boys. This home was the scene of many summer outings. The green hills echoed the gay laughter of the young visitors, and Mrs. Moore's happy family. There was an Indian village near them where the Indians lived in the most primitive style.[3] They were

3. "A few Indians continued to live quietly in various places in Central Louisiana. While passing through Marksville in the 1860s a correspondent for the New Orleans *Crescent* said that Indians on little ponies were a

not at that time the wards of the nation, but they made and executed their own laws. They were of the Choctaw tribe, were friendly and docile, and gave no trouble to their white neighbors. They had little patches of corn and the women wove beautiful baskets of cane splints dyed many bright colors. These baskets were really works of art, and there was always a ready market for them.

The men were successful hunters. They sold the game and also the deer skins. I think they had a secret method of dressing these skins, for the buckskins dressed by them were superior in beauty and durability to any I ever saw.

Mr. and Mrs. Moore were always kind to these poor creatures, and generously gave them provisions and clothes. It was not unusual for a hungry Indian to stop at their door and boldly ask for dinner. They were never turned away.

Choctaw Joe was a frequent visitor at the farm. He made blow-guns for the little boys, and sometimes brought to them the bows and arrows so dear to a boy's heart. This whole family felt an interest in Joe.

One day during the War, when the oldest son was on the far flung battle line in Virginia and Mr. Moore, who was too old for war service, was away from home, Joe came to the front steps, and solemnly said, "Joe hungry; want dinner." Mrs. Moore had a plate heaped with good things for Joe's dinner, and had the cook make some coffee for him. He ate his dinner with great relish, and when he had finished, he looked at Mrs. Moore with great, gloomy black eyes whose expression was unfathomable,

---

common sight. Furthermore, he said they were 'superior-looking Indians', and that they went forth once a year with others from tribes in adjoining parishes to join in a great ball play with the Choctaws from Rapides and elsewhere." Elaine H. Brister, *Once Upon A River: A History of Pineville, Louisiana* (Baton Rouge, 1968), p. 24. Choctaw lands lay on Bayou Boeuf. *Northwest Louisiana Memoirs*, p. 527.

and said, "Well, Joe eat dinner with you no more." Mrs. Moore asked, "Why, Joe. Are you going away?" His reply was, "Joe eat no more." Asked the second time "Why?" he said, "the Indians, he kill Joe." With that he seated himself on the lowest step with his gun across his knees, and his hunting knife at his belt.

Mrs. Moore, thought she had not understood him, but he would not talk any more, but sat quietly awaiting his executioners. After a time a party of Indians came to the gate and called Joe. He gathered his gun into his hands and quietly walked to the gate and joined the Indians. They went in a dignified manner into the wood not far from the house, so near in fact that Mrs. Moore heard the report of the gun when poor Joe paid with his life for whatever savage law he had broken. They buried him there at the place of his execution. They buried him with the honors of war, for they placed his gun and his knife in the grave with him.

The white people never knew what his offense was. There were no witnesses except the party of Indians, but they allowed the knowledge of his burial rites to be known. After their grief for Joe was not so fresh, the two little boys of the Moore family determined to dig up Joe's rifle. They persuaded themselves that Joe did not need the gun and they wanted so very much to get a gun and go to the war. They were only very little boys, but they had heard so much talk of war and guns, and then they reminded themselves that "Brother went to the War; so of course it was right for them to go to." Feeling sure that their mother would not permit them to go out into the woods to Joe's grave, they kept their own council but secured a spade, and kept it in readiness for a time when they could slip off in safety.

One night when there was company in the house, the children were hurried off to bed. After they thought it was safe to embark on their long planned expedition they crawled out a back window, secured the spade, and boldly set off for the grave of their friend. They kept their courage up as best they could.

Arriving at the scene of Joe's execution, they cautiously thrust the spade into the soft sandy soil. After a few minutes work they were overcome by memories of Joe and fears of the Haunts that Aunt Caroline, the cook, had told them about. They almost decided to give up and go home. But they felt that they must have the gun, so went to work with renewed vigor; then the silence of the night was broken by a harsh, sepulchral voice saying, "Whoo! Whoo! Whoo! Ah!" Dear me, how those small boys did run! Dragging the spade after them, they crawled in the window, crept into bed, and shivered with fear till a late hour. They told no one of their expedition. They made several other attempts to possess themselves of this gun, but there were so many awful noises in the woods at night that their hearts grew sick with fear, and the War was over before they were old enough to go to war or bold enough to get the gun.

That rifle has been rusting in the ground for more than sixty years, and today no one living knows where this lonely grave is. The plumey pines which sang a solemn requiem so many years have been cut away, and the denuded hills are stark and naked, a monument to the ruthlessness of man.

X

The Secret

There is one thing I have never told. In my heart of hearts, I have always had a love of high adventure, and even though sometimes it has been deeply overlain with humdrum cares of everyday, I have all the while possessed a rare secret which has never lost the power to thrill me. It has whispered to me from folded household linen; laughed out at me unexpectedly from my mending basket; danced before my eyes in gleaming motes of dust stirred up by my broom. It is a thread of purple-and-gold running through the commonplace fabric of my entire life. Now that I have decided to set it down on paper, I shall begin at the beginning and tell it all.

One day, when I was yet a little girl, a teacher from "out in the pinewoods" came to our house for dinner. He and Pere were great friends, and always had much to talk about. But today he seemed unusually serious. He was going away, and there was something important he wanted to tell Pere before he left. After midday dinner they took their chairs to the cool open hall, and settled down with their pipes.

Professor Dane began by saying that though he was a poor man, he held the key to great wealth. "But I have never been man enough to lift the key and turn it," he said sadly. "Now that I am getting old, it is too late. But I want to pass it on to a younger man who may be able to make use of it." He was haunted by the possibility of dying and his secret being buried with him. He had no family, and as he held Pere in great esteem, he wanted to give it to him. I will let the old teacher tell his own story—I can hear every inflection of my father's voice as he repeated it over and over to us:

Some years ago I was teaching school in Sabine Parish. While getting acquainted with the people of the neighborhood, I found a poor old Frenchman living alone in a little cabin, in direst poverty. He had always been so secretive that the kindly people of the community did not realize his destitute condition. He had married a loose woman who spent everything he had and then left him. This rather prejudiced his neighbors against him. Now he was old, sick, and not able to work, but he still resented anyone's prying into his affairs, as he considered the questioning of the naturally curious country people about him.

His was a pitiable case, so I helped him all I could. By not asking him questions when I took him his food, I seemed to gain his confidence. However, he never told me anything of himself or of his life until the very last.

One day, just a week before the closing of my school, I went to take old man Bouvier—that was the Frenchman's name—some coffee. I found him very feeble; so I boiled water and dripped coffee—black, black—as he liked it. He drank only a little. It was evident that he was greatly perturbed, as if trying to decide some momentous question.

He asked me to take a little bucket to the spring and get some cool water. He said to take another bucket along and bring it back full of white sand. This puzzled me. I thought that the poor old creature's mind was wandering, but nevertheless humored him by bringing the sand.

He drank a little of the water, then sat up and carefully spread the sand on the floor. On its smooth surface, he drew what looked to be a map. He then said, in his broken English, that he was going to tell me something he had never told a living soul before. His black eyes were glittering now and his mind seemed perfectly clear.

"You have heard of Lafitte?" he asked.

"Yes," I said.

"Then listen to what I have to say." This caution was unnecessary. He had my breathless attention. It would be impossible for me to tell his story in his own words, but this is the substance of it.

Some time in 1814, one of Lafitte's ships had made a successful raid on a Spanish galleon, and was heading in toward Barataria heavily laden with loot. At that time Lafitte had fallen into ill repute, and his comings and goings were being closely watched by the minions of the law.

Presently this ship was sighted by a government vessel which set out in hot pursuit. But Lafitte's boat merely sailed into one of those shallow bays with which he and his men were so familiar, and were soon lost to sight. The crew of the government boat, not knowing the channel, dared not follow for fear of running aground. And it would have been nothing short of foolhardy for men to put off in rowboats to take up the chase. So the government vessel stood in the offing three days, waiting for the supposedly trapped pirate crew to venture out. But little did they know what was going on behind the screen of twisted live-oaks on a long narrow shell island! Lafitte's men, deeming it wise to dispose of their treasure as quickly as possible, decided to bury it. They selected a spot on an island across the bay from their pursuers. In the loose sand they soon dug a great hole. They hastily constructed a box of hand hewn live-oak boards two inches thick. The box was exactly three by three by three feet, and they laid in the golden doubloons to within two inches of the top. The remaining space was filled in with jewels. They then nailed up the box and buried it, so that the top was six feet beneath the surface of the ground.

Of course it was necessary to mark the spot in some way. They had located it midway between three live-oaks, which formed almost a perfect triangle. On two of these they cut out a deep chip. The other they cut down, so that it fell directly across the spot where the box was buried.

Having made their treasure safe until they could return for it, Lafitte's men now turned their thoughts toward escape. Slipping out by a hidden bayou, they followed devious waterways until they came out into the Mississippi River. But ill fortune seemed to follow them, for they were again sighted by a government vessel, overhauled, and all killed but five. These five plunged overboard, but only one reached land.

Soon after this Lafitte's band was broken up, most of the men leaving the state with their leader. But the one survivor of the captured vessel wanted to remain in Louisiana, so he just went off to a place where he was not known.

Here old man Bouvier's voice became indistinct, and he mumbled for a minute or two. Then, seeming to come too himself, he straightened up and fixed me with his glittering eyes.

Pointing to the sand map, he said clearly, "See this crescent-shaped bay? That is the bay. And this "—he pointed again—" Cheniere Coronada, is the island. Remember the name." He tapped with his stick. "There lies the treasure! No one in all the world knows where it is but that one man." He looked wildly about him, then his voice dropped to an intense whisper. *"I know—for I am that man!"*

The old Frenchman fell back exhausted and refused to talk any more. After studying his strange map carefully, impressing it on my memory, I swept the sand out with a broken brush.

The next morning the old man was found dead in his cabin. As no one could learn anything about him, he was buried, and thus ended the chapter.

But his strange story had made a deep impression on me. I had very little money, but I felt that I must at least find out if his fabulous island really existed. For fear of injuring my reputation as a sane and respectable school teacher, I never attempted to get anyone to go with me.

That was in May 1855. I went down to the Gulf Coast, and, after considerable inquiry, found that Cheniere Coronada was a real island, instead of the figment of an old Frenchman's fevered brain. I finally engaged a man with a boat to carry me to the island.

A few people lived in this isolated spot, but as they spoke only a French patois, I could not converse with them. They seemed to regard me with great suspicion and enmity. I was enjoined from searching in the daytime, but waited for nightfall. On the second night, the moon rose early and I could see clearly. To my joy, I found two very large live-oaks, and with them forming a perfect triangle, the remains of a stump. But my joy was short-lived, for, turning uneasily, I saw a man slip behind a tree. Then a shot rang out, and I heard the whine of a bullet. I fled to the beach, where I succeeded in engaging a man to take me to the mainland. To remain longer would surely have been throwing my life away.

I had just enough money to get back home. Having been most unfortunate in financial matters since, I have never been able to try again.

Professor Dane seemed to think this closed his story, and only shook his head when Pere urged him to renew the search. He said he was considered too old to teach longer, so he would have to live very carefully to eke out an existence on his little savings. Pere was very much moved by what he had related, and assured Professor Dane that if he located the treasure, half of it was his.

The old teacher then took my father to a smooth place in the yard, and drew a map in the sand, exactly as the Frenchman had done. They went over and over it until Pere had learned the names and locations. They were afraid to trust it to paper, for fear it would get lost and someone else find it. Professor Dane left the neighborhood the next day, and we never saw him again.

It was the fall of 1867, and Pere, like almost everyone else in the South, was very poor. Since the war, he had been restless, hopeless, miserable. He was a young man, and the old teacher's story fired his imagination. Mere, as full of life and love of adventure as he, rather encouraged him in taking up the search for "Lafitte's Box," as they came to speak of it.

Before starting, however, he did take the precaution to go down into Sabine Parish and make inquiries concerning Professor Dane. He found that he was highly thought of in the community where he had taught. As an example of his kind-heartedness, they told how the teacher had befriended a cranky old Frenchman named Bouvier, and cared for him until he died. Of course Pere came back from this trip more excited than ever.

Soon after this he went down to New Orleans on the steam-boat to sell his cotton. While there, he learned what he could about the coast country, and the cost of renting a small boat. When he sold his cotton and returned home, he and Mere decided to stake what cash they had in a gamble for riches.

Pere did not want to go alone, so decided to take his old friend, John Readhimer, into his confidence. He made a trip up to the sand hills in Natchitoches Parish for this purpose. When he told his story, Mr. Readhimer became so enthusiastic he begged my father to let him go in with him, share and share alike on both expenses and findings. This was agreed on, and they got off as soon as possible.

When they reached the coast they rented a little lugger and sailed to their island. They wanted a boat in readiness to leave should danger threaten. They took a pilot who knew the waters, and had no trouble in finding Cheniere Coronada.

After several days search, they located the required triangle: one wind-wrecked live-oak, the dead and bare trunk of a sec-ond, and the almost indistinguishable remains of another stump [paper torn] into a dim scar on the living tree, and found that a big [paper torn] had been cut out many years before. By that time day was near [paper torn] to be content with standing in the center of the triangle, gloating, "Just wait till tonight, John!" But his hopes never came to fruition.

There was on the island a Negro who had run away some years before, while a slave. He had belonged to English-speaking people, and in his pleasure at being able to talk to someone in this language, he had made friends with Mr. Readhimer and Pere. He had kept his comings and goings a secret. That day, he crawled into their camp, and called to my father.

He tremblingly told him that the people on the island had planned to kill the two of them that night, and begged them to leave. With the hot-headedness of the young, my father wanted to stay and fight it out. But Mr. Readhimer, an older man, refused to remain. They left at once, planning to return next year.

In the poverty and bitterness of Reconstruction days, Pere's trip in search of golden doubloons was of necessity put off from year to year, until death cheated him of accomplishing his dream. But I was my father's own child, and his dream lived on in my heart.

Mere, Sister, and I often discussed this fascinating subject. In fact, Bouvier's Box came to be a sort of family by-word with us—though always a carefully cherished secret. When we had to deny ourselves some longed-for pleasure, one would say with a mysterious smile, "Never mind! Just wait till we find Bouvier's Box!"

So in-and-out through the years was woven this shining thread. When I married, I tried to get my husband interested, but he quoted me those wise old platitudes, "A bird in the hand is worth two in the bush," and all the rest. Of course he was right. We had our little baby to think of, and there was no money with which to fit out a treasure hunt.

The years flowed by, but Bouvier's Box never grew less clear in my mind. My second husband merely laughed at my "pretty tale" so I never discussed it with him any more. But when Sister and I were together we often mentioned it. Then my grandchildren came, and for a time, filled all my thoughts. When I became a widow again, my grandson spent a great deal of time with me. I told him the treasure story, and he was fascinated. He made me tell it over and over, and, at the end, he would always say, "When I get big, Grandma, we'll go find Bouvier's Box, won't we?"

Then he was grown. One day, on some whim of the moment, I told him that the story was all true. He must have inherited his grandfather's high heart, for he became very much excited over it. He asked my consent to his taking a few of his closest friends into our confidence.

A little later, he came in to tell me that his friends had begged to be allowed to become partners in the enterprise. But best of all, he said, he had stumbled on a man who had invented a new method for detecting buried metals. They were to take this machine along.

That was some time ago. Now everything has been worked out to the last detail, and all is in readiness for departure. They had a launch engaged and fitted out. Now, indeed, am I living in a dream. Some of my friends and relatives were horrified when they heard that I was going. The idea of a woman my age taking part in such a wild goose chase!

As if I would let them go without me! It is not often in life that one sees a lovely dream crystallize into reality. I shall not let such an opportunity slip through my fingers simply because some old sit-by-the-fire thinks it shocking. If we find the treasure I will be able to help those I love. If a hurricane catches us in the Gulf and I am drowned, I will at least have died on the [paper torn] of a glorious adventure.

The plans all sound too modern. I do not listen when they tell me. To me it all belongs to the past, is bound up too closely with the years that are gone—a part of "Dear dead days beyond recall. It is all very beautiful to me—like the last lovely glow of the sky when day is nearing its close.

At last I am to see mysterious islands set in winding streamways, wind-wrecked trees in significant patterns, sparkling waves on crescent beaches. My old pulses throb. I find myself repeating, "three feet by three feet by three feet . . . !"

And I'm going in the morning!

(Dosia Williams Lewis Moore was born in South Carolina, and at three years of age came to Louisiana with her parents. She was married to Albert D. Lewis in 1878. Mr. Lewis died in 1882. They had one son, A. D. Lewis. Later she married W. S. Moore. She died December 21, 1938 at Alexandria, Louisiana and is buried at Mount Olivet cemetery, Pineville, Louisiana. *Alexandria Daily Town Talk*, December 31, 1938.)

Index